A HOUSE DIVIDED

Rediscovering Unity in the Last days

JUEL MENDEZ

A HOUSE DIVIDED
Copyright © 2025 by Juel Mendez
All rights reserved.

No part of this publication may be reproduced, stored in a retrieval system, or transmitted in any form or by any means—electronic, mechanical, photocopying, recording, or otherwise—without the prior written permission of the publisher, except in the case of brief quotations used for reviews, academic work, or noncommercial teaching, provided full credit is given.

Unless otherwise noted, Scripture quotations are taken from the following translations:

King James Version (KJV) — Public domain
Legacy Standard Bible (LSB) — © The Lockman Foundation and Three Sixteen Publishing. Used by permission. All rights reserved.
New American Standard Bible (NASB) — © The Lockman Foundation 1995/2020. Used by permission. All rights reserved.
English Standard Version (ESV) — © Crossway, a publishing ministry of Good News Publishers. Used by permission. All rights reserved.

This work is a theological exhortation, not a substitute for Scripture, pastoral oversight, or Spirit-led accountability within the local church. It is offered to the Body of Christ as a watchman's call—one that seeks not to wound, but to warn. Not to divide, but to urge faithful reformation. Any critique is directed at ideas, not individuals.

The views expressed are solely those of the author and do not represent any specific denomination, ecclesiastical body, or institution. Readers are urged to examine all claims in light of Scripture and in the counsel of mature believers who fear the Lord.

First Edition: August 1, 2025
Print ISBN: 978-1-7360535-0-8
E-Book ISBN: 978-1-7360535-1-5
Published by: The Watchman's Seal
Website: www.bearonesburden.com
Contact: info@bearonesburden.com
Cover and Interior Design: Juel Mendez

To download the free companions to this book, visit: juelmendez.com/books-christian-apologetics

CONTENTS

The Watchman's Charge v
Epigraph vii
Acknowledgements ix
Preface xi
Introduction xvii
Chapter 1 1
Chapter 2 29
Chapter 3 47
Chapter 4 73
Chapter 5 99
Chapter 6 133
Chapter 7 161
Chapter 8 181
Chapter 10 221
A Watchman's Final Question 237
Appendix 241
Endnotes 247
Bibliography 269
About the Author 271
Also by 273

The Watchman's Charge

A Commissioning for the Defender of Truth

I do not argue to win — I speak to warn.

I do not defend an idea — I defend a Kingdom.

I do not fear opposition — I fear silence when the truth is required.

I am not driven by applause, platform, or pride.

I answer to the King of Truth.

I serve truth even when it convicts.

I expose deception, but I do not disgrace the Gospel.

I study to show myself approved.

I reason from the Word.

I respond with wisdom, gentleness, and fire.

I am a burden-bearer.

I carry the weight of truth in a world allergic to it.

I investigate the lies, expose the idols, and point to the cross.

I am not ashamed of the Gospel.

I stand in a generation that sits in compromise.

I speak where others whisper.

I love without retreating.

I preach without twisting.

For I do not contend for relevance —

I contend for revelation.

I am a Watchman.

I bear the burden.

I sound the warning.

And I speak as one who will give an account.

For Ezekiel 33:7 says,

"I have made you a watchman… so hear the word I speak and give them warning from Me."

I am a Watchman.

Epigraph

"(For the weapons of our warfare are not carnal, but mighty through God to the pulling down of strong holds;)

Casting down imaginations, and every high thing that exalteth itself against the knowledge of God, and bringing into captivity every thought to the obedience of Christ."

— 2 Corinthians 10:4–5

Acknowledgements

First and foremost, I give all glory to the Lord Jesus Christ, the Word made flesh, who not only redeemed me, but patiently taught me to discern between man's theology and His truth. He is the reason this book exists. To Him belong all honor, all wisdom, and all authority.

To the Holy Spirit—who gently corrected me, trained me through Scripture, and awakened my calling to apologetics—not to divide the Body, but to help restore it. Thank You for guiding me back to what is written.

To my family, who walked with me through this journey—thank you for your endurance, patience, and grace. Your prayers and faithfulness gave me the space to wrestle, to study, and to write.

To the brothers and sisters in Christ who encouraged me to speak when it would have been easier to stay silent—this book is as much your courage as it is my conviction.

To the many pastors and elders I sat under—some who taught truth, and others who inadvertently helped reveal error—thank you. Your words, even when they hurt, drove me deeper into the Word of

God. You stirred the questions that gave birth to this calling.

To those who responded with misunderstanding or dismissal, I hold no bitterness. What was intended to halt a conversation became the catalyst for this book. May the Lord use even that for His glory.

To those who are reading this—searching for answers, grieving over division in the Church, or feeling isolated for asking hard questions—this book is for you. You are not alone. Stay grounded in the Word, and let the truth speak for itself.

Lastly, I dedicate this work to the local Church—not a name, not a building, but the Body of Christ across all nations, denominations, and languages. May we return to the simplicity that is in Christ, the authority of Scripture, and the unity for which He prayed.

Soli Deo Gloria.
— Juel Mendez

Preface

This book began with a question:
If the Word of God is clear, why is the Church so divided?

That question didn't come from intellectual curiosity. It came from the battlefield of experience—after years of sermons that didn't match the Scriptures. Of asking sincere questions and being met with silence—or worse, deflection. Of being told to sit down when I simply wanted to understand what God had already said.

Over two decades, I sat under many leaders. I visited many churches. I watched denominations drift deeper into systems, rituals, and frameworks that often elevated theological labels over the Gospel itself. I didn't leave because I wanted to wander. I left because I was searching—searching for the simplicity that is in Christ.

What I found was this: many Christians love Jesus, but they've been discipled by their denomination. Their faith is filtered—not always through Scripture, but through systems built around it. And when those systems are challenged, even gently, the result is rarely humility. It's often rejection.

Eventually, I reached a moment of confrontation.

Not rebellion—but biblical conviction. I asked questions rooted in the Word, spoken in love, aimed at unity. What I received in return was dismissal—not because I denied Christ, but because I questioned tradition. Not because I caused division, but because I exposed it.

I never wanted to write this book out of bitterness. I wrote it because silence would have been disobedience.

A Watchman's Awakening

For years, I struggled with what I saw in churches around the world. I wrestled with contradictions, fragmented doctrine, and how many well-meaning believers treated theology like tribal armor—using it to defend positions rather than sharpen understanding.

Eventually, I stopped asking leaders for answers and started letting Scripture interpret itself. And when I did, the fog began to clear. The contradictions weren't in the Word—they were in the way we had learned to handle it.

That realization became my assignment: not to deconstruct the Church—but to call it back to clarity. Not to create more noise—but to recover the voice of the Watchman.

The tools that guide this book—the framework I now teach others—came through fire, prayer, and relentless testing. I now use five interpretive tests to guard against confusion and to filter every teaching through the Word alone:

- Language Consistency
- Immediate Context Integrity
- Historical-Cultural Context
- Theological Consistency

- Christocentric Alignment

Each is explored further in the Appendix. But understand this: they are not intellectual strategies. They are survival tools. They were birthed to protect the flock, not to impress scholars.

A Return to the Church's Purpose

The early Church faced division. But the apostles didn't avoid it—they addressed it. They reasoned from the Scriptures. They corrected false teachers. They refined doctrine without losing fellowship.

Today, we often do the opposite. We either argue endlessly—or remain silent in the name of "peace." Neither option honors Christ. He prayed that we would be one—not in emotion, not in denomination, but in Him.

This book calls the Church to return to its assignment:

- To feed the flock with knowledge and understanding (Jeremiah 3:15)
- To guard against clever philosophies (Colossians 2:8)
- To elevate Christ, not personality or platform
- To restore unity through shared obedience to Scripture—not silence

In some pulpits today, the teacher has been replaced by the celebrity. The prophet has been replaced by the planner. And the Word has been replaced by interpretation. This book exists to sound the alarm—and then hand you a trowel to rebuild.

You're Asking the Same Questions...

If you've ever sat in a church wondering why one passage is preached and another is ignored... If you've felt tension between your Bible and your tradition... If you've been told to stop asking questions when you're simply trying to understand the truth...

Then this book is for you.

It will not give you every answer. But it will help you test every teaching:

- Does it align with the plain meaning of Scripture?
- Does it exalt Christ—or elevate man?
- Does it produce holiness—or hierarchy?
- Does it unify around truth—or divide around tradition?

Let us be Bereans again. Let us search the Scriptures daily (Acts 17:11). Let us guard the simplicity that is in Christ (2 Corinthians 11:3). Let us return to the prayer Jesus prayed before the cross—not just for truth, but for unity in that truth (John 17).

This is a call to shepherds: return to the Word. A call to teachers: speak again with clarity. A call to the Body: test everything. Rebuild the wall. Hold fast to the Gospel.

Not the Gospel of manipulation. Not the Gospel of emotionalism. Not the Gospel of man-made systems. But the Gospel of the Word. The Word made flesh. The Word that saves. The Word that unites.

Solus Christus. Sola Scriptura. Sola Gratia. Let us not only remember it. Let us return to it.

So please hear what I am saying—and do not hear what I am not. This book is not against passion in worship. It is not against tradition when it submits to truth. It is not against questions—as long as they lead us back to the Word, not further into speculation.

What it confronts is a quiet and dangerous exchange:

- Where the emotional replaces the exegetical
- Where interpretation replaces instruction
- Where performance masks the absence of sound doctrine

We have allowed the grey areas of secondary doctrines—when left undefined or made central—to fog the vision of the Church.

In the name of spiritual liberty, we have confused the body. In the name of relevance, we have diluted the Word. In the name of unity, we have tolerated deception.

This is not merely an issue of preference or perspective. It is an issue of discipleship. It is an issue of authority. It is an issue of truth.

When pulpits blur what God has made clear, the sheep wander. When leaders exalt grey revelation over black-and-white commands, false gospels are born. And when the people of God no longer know how to test the spirits, they will follow anything with a microphone.

This book, *A House Divided*, is not a call to fight—but to discern. Not a manifesto for rebellion—but a manual for return.

It will challenge not only what we believe—but how we came to believe it. It will ask whether we are submitted to the Word—or to a voice we've mistaken for it.

This is not about settling every debate. It is about ensuring that the debate never replaces the foundation.

Let us rediscover what the Church was meant to be: A house built on the rock. A pillar and ground of the truth (1 Timothy 3:15). A body joined not by style, denomination, or giftedness —but by the Word made flesh, crucified, risen, and reigning.

May what divides us be cast down. May what unites us be restored. And may the Church once again be known—not by noise, but by truth spoken in love.

—Juel Mendez

Introduction

A cracked wall doesn't collapse all at once. It splits in silence. Slowly. Almost politely.

Such is the state of the Church.

We are not persecuted into weakness—we are divided into it. Not by the world, but by ourselves. By a thousand pulpits proclaiming a thousand truths. By doctrine turned into tribalism. By pastors who shepherd platforms more than people.

Jesus prayed: "that they may all be one." We've repeated His words. We've quoted them on bulletins and banners. But we haven't obeyed them.

And the fracture is no longer theoretical. It's visible. Tangible. Measurable in churches closed, in credibility lost, in a generation more discipled by influencers than elders.

Across the centuries, we've split over predestination and sacraments, over tongues and timelines, over women and worship—and even over who is allowed to wash feet. Some of these matters matter deeply. Others never should have. But when everything becomes a hill to die on, we stop seeing the hill where Christ already did.

This book is not a call to consensus. It's a call to clarity—and to courage. It is not written to settle arguments, but to summon the Watchman. To awaken those who still carry the burden of truth in an age allergic to it.

We will walk through fire. We will face cherished traditions and beloved teachings. We will not emerge without cost. But unity is not optional. It is not sentimental. It is not negotiable.

It is our witness.

And if the Church remains a house divided, we will not stand. Not under pressure. Not in persecution. Not before the returning King.

So the question is not: Will we unify? The question is: Will we be found faithful when He comes?

1

The Fault Line Beneath The Church

The Illusion of Stability

How the Church Mistook Stillness for Strength

A wall does not fall in a day. It weakens in silence. It shifts by degrees. What seems immovable on the outside may already be betraying hidden fractures within. A temple may gleam with gold and incense. It may shimmer with history and echo with tradition. Tourists may marvel. Worshippers may gather. But their footsteps often fall upon a fault line—a thin, near-invisible crack running beneath polished marble. Then one day, the ground groans. The wall collapses. And only then come the questions. Only then does the blame follow.

But the fracture was always there.

So it is with the Church

We have mistaken the absence of noise for the presence

of health. We've confused growth with strength. We've confused activity with alignment. And most dangerously, we've renamed division with softer, less convicting labels:

"denominations,"
"streams,"
"traditions."

We've turned these categories into badges of identity—sometimes even into walls of separation. We wear our distinctives like armor. Or worse—like pride. The sermons continue. The songs still rise. The buildings still fill. But the fault line beneath us runs deep.

We speak the name of Christ while living in houses divided. We preach about oneness in the Spirit while celebrating the proliferation of theological camps, content creators, and doctrinal brands. And we tell ourselves this is normal.

To be clear: not every difference is disobedience. Romans 14 teaches us to bear with one another in disputable matters—areas of conscience, not core doctrine. The Jerusalem council in Acts 15 modeled this balance: clarity on essentials, grace on non-essentials, and unity in mission. But what began as godly diversity has too often hardened into rivalry. We've lost the ability to distinguish between a hill to die on and a hill to walk over together.

Where Did the Illusion Begin?

The illusion of stability began where all spiritual erosion begins: with good intentions left unchecked by humility. When Constantine legalized Christianity in the fourth century, the Church moved from caves to cathedrals. A persecuted people became a powerful institution. With power came privilege—and with privilege, the temptation to build walls rather than cultivate roots.

Then came the creeds and councils—many necessary and God-ordained, but each carrying the risk of shifting from unity in truth to control in structure. By the time the Great Schism tore the Church between East and West in 1054, it was clear: unity could fracture even when the buildings remained intact.

The Reformation in the 16th century was vital—a return to Scripture and salvation by grace. But with it came a new danger: every correction eventually spawned its own sub-corrections. Each movement produced more movements. Each reformer, more reformations. Protest itself became a model.

And now?

We have inherited centuries of splintered theology, divided denominations, and competing tribes of thought. And we call it "diversity" instead of what it really is: doctrinal drift, relational rupture, and spiritual disorientation. The illusion of stability began when we confused correction with division and never reconciled the two.

And yet—even amid the fractures—God has not been absent. In every denomination, however flawed, the Gospel has still gone forth. His Word has not returned void. Missionaries have been sent. Souls have been saved. The global spread of Christianity is not proof that division is harmless—but it is evidence that God's providence can work even through a fractured vessel.

Why Has It Continued?

Because the alternative is costly. Unity requires repentance. It requires humility. It demands that we lay down our brand in order to raise up the Body.

Division, however, is comfortable. It allows us to stay in our camps. It allows us to keep our pulpits. It allows us to measure health by agreement rather than by truth.

A HOUSE DIVIDED

Division persists because it serves our pride. We fear being misunderstood more than we fear misrepresenting Christ. We defend theological nuance while ignoring theological fruit. And so we elevate:

- Cleverness over clarity
- Systems over Scripture
- Experience over obedience

We do it because it makes us feel secure. It gives us identity. It allows us to compare ourselves—not to Christ, but to the church down the street. And in our fear of confrontation, we've made peace with fragmentation.

> *"They have healed the wound of my people lightly, saying, 'Peace, peace,' when there is no peace."*
> *—Jeremiah 6:14*

This false peace—the illusion of stability—keeps the wall upright just long enough for the next generation to inherit its weight.

Why We Must Change It

Because the shaking has already begun. Jesus didn't pray for harmony of style or surface-level niceness. He prayed for oneness in truth.

> *"Sanctify them in the truth; Your World is truth... that they may all be one."—John 17:17, 21*

This wasn't a poetic closing to a prayer. It was His mission strategy. His credibility in the world was to be revealed by the unity of His Body. But we have not broken His prayer—we have simply ignored it.

> *"Every kingdom divided against itself is laid waste, and no city or house divided against itself will stand."–Matthew 12:25*

These are not warnings to be glossed over. They are spiritual laws of gravity. A house divided will not stand. A wall ignored will eventually fall. And a Church that cannot agree on what matters most will lose its voice—even if it keeps its attendance.

The Restoration Begins with Us

The question is not, "Can unity exist?" The question is,

"Are we willing to pay the cost for it?"

It begins with:

- A return to the Scriptures—not filtered through systems, but studied with fear and trembling.
- A willingness to confront error—not with arrogance, but with tears.
- A rejection of spiritual tribalism—where Christ is claimed, but systems are enthroned.

It begins with Watchmen sounding the alarm and builders returning to the wall. We do not need another rebranding of the Church. We need rebuilding. We need to inspect the cracks, to lay aside what divides us, and to return to what unites us eternally:

One Lord.

One faith.

> One baptism.
>
> One Spirit.
>
> One God and Father of all.
>
> —Ephesians 4:4-6

The wall may still be standing. But unless we remove the illusion, it will not stand much longer.

> Let the Watchman speak.
> Let the Church awaken.
> Let the rebuilding begin.

Division Is Not Just Unfortunate—It's Rebellion

We have been given a warning—from Christ, from Paul, and from the crumbling wall beneath us. We call doctrinal fracture a "difference of opinion." We package division in polite terms: tradition, preference, stream, movement. But Jesus never softened His expectations for unity. He didn't suggest it. He prayed for it.

> "That they may all be one...so that the world may believe that You sent Me."—John 17:21

This was not sentimental poetry. It was strategic intercession. Jesus tied the credibility of the Gospel to the unity of His followers. When we fragment the Body, we do not merely disagree with each other—we actively undermine the witness of Christ.

Where We Fall Short: Treating Division Like a Cosmetic Issue

We've fallen into a dangerous kind of theological apathy. We've convinced ourselves that disunity is survivable—that as long as we preach Jesus, it doesn't matter how splintered we become over the rest.

But Jesus said otherwise:

> *"Every kingdom divided against itself is brought to desolation, and every city or house divided against itself will not stand."—Matthew 12:25*

We often quote this when speaking about culture or national politics. But Jesus was addressing a principle that applies to any spiritual body—especially His Church. When we act as if doctrinal fragmentation is normal, we deny what He declared to be fatal.

A divided Church is not stable. It is staggering toward collapse.

And yet, how easily we say:

> *"It's just a doctrinal disagreement."*
> *"It's not a Gospel issue."*
> *"We're all on the same team."*

But look at our team. We've turned the Gospel into a tribal brand, with every corner of Christendom defending its stream with more passion than defending the unity of the faith. We've traded Christ's intercession for theological isolation.

Why Paul's Command Still Matters

Paul didn't ignore false teaching. He was relentless in his defense of the Gospel. But he also rebuked the spirit of division—even when truth was involved.

> *"I appeal to you, brothers, by the name of our Lord Jesus Christ, that all of you agree...and that there be no division among you, but that you be*

> *united in the same mind and the same judgment."*
> *—1 Corinthians 1:10*

This was not about ignoring error. It was about the posture of the Church.

The Corinthian believers weren't just fighting over sin. They were dividing over personalities: "I follow Paul... I follow Apollos... I follow Cephas." It was a split of devotion disguised as discernment.

Paul's solution was simple: return to Christ as the center. He wasn't asking them to erase their differences. He was calling them to submit those differences to the Cross.

But in our generation, we often do the opposite. We don't return to Christ. We defend the system that affirms us. We quote our favorite pastor more than we quote Scripture. We become followers of ideas instead of disciples of the Word.

Paul's appeal is still echoing: "Be united." Not by strategy. Not by branding. But by the Gospel itself.

Jesus Is the Cornerstone—And He's Still Speaking

We must remember what the Church is built on:

> "Behold, I am laying in Zion a stone, a tested stone, a precious cornerstone, of a sure foundation: whoever believes will not be in haste."—Isaiah 28:16

> "The stone that the builders rejected has become the cornerstone."—Psalm 118:22

> "For no one can lay a foundation other than

that which is laid, which is Jesus Christ."
—*1 Corinthians 3:11*

Jesus is not one of many supports in the Christian life—He is the foundation. He is the cornerstone that defines everything else. And He is still speaking.

Every time the Church elevates tradition over truth, He speaks. Every time believers divide over systems He never instituted, He speaks. Every time we defend our theological tribe while ignoring our theological fruit, He warns us.

His warning is not hidden. It's in plain sight.

When He prayed for unity in John 17, He wasn't offering a preference—He was revealing divine design. When He declared that a divided house cannot stand, He wasn't giving advice. He was describing spiritual law.

We can either align with His voice—or ignore it and collapse.

Division: The Enemy's Comfort Zone

We often act like division only harms our image. But it does more than that. It doesn't just confuse the world. It doesn't just frustrate the faithful. It comforts the enemy.

Satan doesn't need to silence the Church. He only needs to distract it long enough to keep it fragmented. He loves when we quarrel over Calvinism, gifts of the Spirit, end times charts, or worship formats—because while we fight each other, we forget the mission.

And while we forget the mission, he remains unopposed. We are not storming the gates of hell. We're building moats around our theological camps.

A HOUSE DIVIDED

Returning to the Cornerstone

Unity will not come through ecumenical agreements or surface-level collaborations. It will come when the Church—across every tradition—returns to the Cornerstone.

It will come when we:

- Lay down our pride
- Submit our systems to Scripture
- Admit that we have tolerated division for too long
- Confess that some of our cherished labels are not fruit—they are flesh

It will come when the cry of our heart is no longer

"Who's right?"

but rather:

"Are we being faithful to Christ—together?"

The Final Plea: Repent Before Collapse

Division is not just unfortunate. It is rebellion. Not rebellion against a movement or a method—but against the very prayer of Jesus and the structure of His Church. We will not endure the shaking to come if we are still standing on broken ground.

> *"Make every effort to keep the unity of the Spirit through the bond of peace."—Ephesians 4:3*

This is not a suggestion. It is a command. So let us repent. Let us return to the foundation. Let us rebuild the walls of the Church with truth, humility, and love. Because unless we return to the Cornerstone—we will collapse.

The Myth of Harmless Schism

How We've Traded Apostolic Fear for Brand Loyalty

The early Church was not free from controversy. They wrestled. They disagreed. They debated fiercely over doctrine, practice, and identity. But their goal was always unity in truth—not victory in debate.

The Apostle Paul withstood Peter to his face—not to shame him, but to preserve the integrity of the Gospel (Galatians 2). The apostles convened in Jerusalem—not to splinter, but to reason together over the Gentile question (Acts 15). When theological tension arose, the response was not retreat. It was correction, clarity, and then continued fellowship.

They did not form rival congregations. They did not build denominations around every dispute. They did not divide to protect their brand—they contended together to preserve the Gospel's witness.

What the apostles treated with trembling, we now treat with marketing.

From Reverence to Rebranding

Contrast that apostolic reverence with the modern Church. Where once the Body feared division, we now franchise it.

The East–West Schism of 1054 split the Church over the filioque clause and papal authority—leaving centuries of unresolved theological tension in its wake. The Reformation, though a necessary call back to the authority of Scripture and salvation by grace, opened the floodgates for a new model: when disagreements arise, create a new church.

That model has not only continued—it has accelerated. Today, there are over 45,000 Protestant denominations worldwide. Some were born out of serious theological disagreement. Many were born out of conflict, personality clashes, or cultural adaptations.

We no longer contend for unity. We default to separation.

We Divide Over Everything

Doctrinal disagreement has become a rite of passage for ministry growth. We plant churches not to multiply the mission—but to escape correction.

We divide over everything:

- Calvinism vs. Arminianism
- Cessationism vs. Continuationism
- Mode of baptism, end times timelines, the role of women, spiritual gifts
- Governance structures, music styles, liturgy, dress codes

Each disagreement spawns a new network. Each offense gives birth to a movement. And under it all lies something dangerous—ego masquerading as conviction.

We quote doctrine, but we defend identity. We raise theological banners, but not to unify the Church—often only to gather our own tribe.

"I follow Paul... I follow Apollos... I follow Cephas."
—1 Corinthians 1:12-13

Paul saw this not as loyalty—but as sectarianism

in disguise. We've repeated Corinth's mistake—but we've added websites, logos, and conference circuits.

Schism Bleeds the Church

Let us be clear: schism is not neutral. It does not simply "allow space" for diversity. It bleeds witness. It fractures authority. It erodes public credibility.

When a watching world sees the Church split into thousands of factions—each claiming to be Spirit-led, Bible-believing, and Gospel-centered—they don't marvel at our theological precision. They question our sincerity. They doubt our unity.

And worse—they are tempted to believe that truth is unknowable, because Christians can't even agree on what it is.

> *"That they may all be one... so that the world may believe that You sent Me."—John 17:21*

Every fracture weakens that witness. Every new splinter clouds that clarity.

We've Built Camps, Not Communion

There's a subtle but damning shift that has occurred in the heart of the Church. We've mistaken system loyalty for Gospel fidelity. We've built camps instead of communion.

We've trained our leaders to defend theological tribes more fiercely than they defend the unity of Christ's Body. Theology is no longer a window to behold Christ—it has become a wall to keep out disagreement.

We quote the Reformers, not realizing that they, too, warned against this spirit. We exalt our denominational distinctives as if they were direct revelations—forgetting that most of them were historical responses, not eternal mandates.

Theological frameworks are helpful. But when they become the lens through which we read the Bible—rather than the servant of the Bible—they become idols in the name of orthodoxy.

The Church Is Bleeding Out

We are bleeding—not because of persecution, but because of infighting.

- While we write blogs critiquing other believers, souls go unreached.
- While we divide over spiritual gifts, we neglect the fruit of the Spirit.
- While we argue over whether the Spirit still moves, we ignore that He is grieved.

The Church was never meant to be a system of disconnected networks. It was meant to be a Body—joined and held together by what every joint supplies (Ephesians 4:16).

Schism weakens the Body at every level. It isolates the arm from the hand. It silences the voice from the ear. And it leaves the feet too weary to go where they are sent.

A Call Back to Apostolic Unity

We must rediscover the fear the apostles had:

- The fear of wounding the Body
- The fear of elevating self over Chris
- The fear of becoming right in theology but wrong in Spirit

This book does not call for theological compromise. It calls for accountability—to Christ, to His Word, and to one another.

Truth still matters. Clarity still matters. Doctrine still matters. But so does oneness.

> *"Make every effort to keep the unity of the Spirit through the bond of peace."—Ephesians 4:3*

Make every effort. Not just to articulate doctrine. But to live it in love—and to guard the unity Christ already secured.

The time for branding the Body is over. The time for rebuilding it—together—has come.

The Blueprint for Oneness

Unity as the Gospel's Witness to the World

If you listen closely to the heart of Jesus before the cross, you will not hear a strategy session. You will not hear a plea for political power, institutional growth, or cultural acceptance. You will hear a prayer—a specific, aching, final prayer:

> *"That they may all be one, just as You, Father, are in Me, and I in You, that they also may be in Us, so that the world may believe that You have sent Me."*
> *—John 17:21*

This prayer is not poetic filler. It is the center of Christ's high priestly intercession. It is the theological and relational blueprint for the Church.

It is not vague. It is not optional. It is not sentimental. It is spiritual architecture—a design that, if ignored, will

A HOUSE DIVIDED

collapse under its own weight. A mandate that ties the effectiveness of the Gospel to the visible oneness of God's people.

More Than a Prayer—A Plea

Jesus prayed this prayer knowing what was coming. He knew Peter would deny. He knew the disciples would scatter. He knew the Church, in the centuries to follow, would be tempted by division, tribalism, and pride.

But He did not pray that His people would agree on every detail. He prayed they would be one—in truth, in Spirit, in fellowship. He prayed for a unity that reflected the eternal oneness of Father and Son.

> *"That they may be one even as We are one."*
> *—John 17:21*

This is not uniformity. This is not compromise. This is supernatural fellowship—birthed by the Spirit, anchored in the truth, and held together by shared allegiance to Christ.

Unity is not just relational. It is missional. It is how the world knows Jesus is real.

We've Misread the Mission

The Church today has become efficient in everything but oneness. We can organize events. We can build networks. We can develop content, plant churches, and expand reach.

But all of it lacks eternal impact if it does not flow from the unity Jesus prayed for.

> *"By this all people will know that you are My*

disciples, if you have love for one another."
—John 13:35

We've replaced love with loyalty to systems. We've replaced oneness with alignment around personalities. We've replaced Christ-centered communion with theological alliances.

And the world is watching. They do not hear a single witness—they hear competing claims. They do not see a unified Church—they see a fractured institution. And they walk away unconvinced.

Jesus never said the world would believe because of our arguments.

He said they would believe because of our oneness.

Oneness Is Not Optional

John 17 is not a suggestion. It is not a prayer we can politely ignore. It is the center of Christ's vision for His Church.

It is the hinge upon which credibility swings. It is the difference between cultural relevance and Kingdom power. It is the mark of discipleship that proves Christ is alive in His people.

This prayer is not theoretical—it is prophetic. And when we divide, we do not merely defy our brothers and sisters—we resist the intercession of Jesus Himself.

How We've Drifted from the Blueprint

We've built churches with good intentions—but on shaky ground. We've erected theological scaffolding, but we've often ignored the cornerstone of oneness.

Here's how it happened:

- We prioritized being right over being reconciled.

- We elevated secondary issues to primary status.
- We allowed personal offense to birth new movements.
- We chose to walk away rather than sit together under the Word.
- We defended truth in a way that abandoned love.

In doing so, we drifted from the blueprint. And the foundation began to crack.

Oneness Is Built on Truth

Make no mistake—unity cannot survive apart from truth. Jesus did not pray for unity at the expense of Scripture. He prayed:

> "Sanctify them in the truth; Your word is truth."
> —John 17:17

Oneness that avoids truth is sentiment. Oneness built on truth is sacred. We must be a people who walk in both clarity and charity—refusing to abandon truth, but also refusing to wield it as a weapon against our own.

This is the narrow road. It is the harder road. But it is the one that Christ walked—and the one He calls us to walk together.

If We Don't Return to the Prayer

The danger is not simply disunity—it is discredit.

The world is not confused by our theology. It is hardened by our division. We have declared that Jesus saves, but we live as if He doesn't unite. We proclaim the Spirit regenerates, but act as if He cannot reconcile. We preach the Cross, but divide at every theological crossroads.

What happens if we do not return to the prayer of Christ? We may continue to build. But we will build in vain.

The Invitation to Align

The blueprint has not changed. John 17 still stands. The Cornerstone is still in place. And Jesus is still interceding. The question is not whether His prayer was powerful. The question is whether we will align with it.

To do so, we must:

- Submit our preferences to His priorities
- Place Scripture above systems
- Relearn how to reason together
- Refuse to break fellowship over what Christ never intended to divide us

Oneness is not idealism. It is obedience. It is the evidence that Christ is in us, and that the Gospel is real. Let the Church return to the blueprint. Let the walls be measured again by what He prayed—not by what we prefer. Let our unity be proof that He is who He says He is. Because the world won't believe until we become one—not in method, but in mission. In truth. In Christ.

We've Accepted Division as Normal

When we made division normal, we lost more than organizational cohesion—we lost witness, weight, and clarity.

- **We lost our collective authority.**
  When the world sees 45,000 denominations,

each claiming to preach Christ, it doesn't see theological richness—it sees confusion.

- **We lost our moral credibility.**
  A divided Church cannot speak with one voice into a world fractured by sin. It cannot call for reconciliation while harboring internal schism.

- **We lost our prophetic power.**
  When believers prioritize their theological stream over the Body, they may speak with passion—but not with heaven's backing.

Division doesn't simply weaken us —it compromises our testimony.

The Path Back: Three Anchors for Unity

If we are to walk together again, we must recover shared foundations.

Unity cannot be restored by campaigns or slogans. It must be rebuilt from the ground up—on three non-negotiable commitments:

1. Shared Submission to Scripture

The Bible must once again become the final authority—not filtered through our systems, but approached with trembling.

It cannot serve as a sourcebook for confirmation bias. It must be the voice that silences all others. And it must be interpreted in community, not in isolation.

When every theological tribe claims Scripture, but interprets it in a vacuum, disunity is inevitable. We must return to the model of Acts 15—opening the Word together, reasoning together, and listening to the Spirit together.

2. Shared Faith in Christ Alone

Jesus is not a mascot for our systems.

He is the center.

We are saved by grace alone, through faith alone, in Christ alone—not through theological clarity or denominational allegiance. If we cannot gather at the foot of the cross, regardless of our secondary differences, we have exchanged the Gospel for a doctrinal club.

True unity does not demand uniform expression. But it demands shared allegiance to the same Lord, the same Savior, the same Gospel.

3. Shared Humility in Disputable Matters

This may be the hardest anchor to reclaim—because it requires death to self.

> *"Clothe yourselves with humility towards one another." — 1 Peter 5:5*

Humility is not silence. It's posture. It's the ability to say, "I may be right in content, but wrong in tone." It's the willingness to hold secondary convictions with clarity and love—not with contempt.

It's refusing to make every disagreement a dividing line. It's recognizing that what unites us is stronger than what tempts to divide us.

Unity Demands Cost

True unity is not built on convenience. It's built on sacrifice. To pursue it, we will have to:

- Dismantle pride
- Shrink our platforms
- Submit our pet doctrines
- Open our doors wider
- Forgive where offense has festered
- And honor brothers and sisters who do not wear our theological badge

This is not spiritual idealism. It is spiritual warfare. Because division is not just a doctrinal issue. It is a heart issue. And unless we confront it with the same urgency that we confront error, it will continue to rot the Body from the inside out.

Unity Is Not Uniformity—It's Fidelity

The call to unity is not a call to sameness. It is a call to Christ-centered fidelity. We are not asked to erase our differences. We are commanded to submit them to the Lordship of Christ. To anchor ourselves in the essentials:

One Lord,

One faith,

One baptism,

One Spirit,

One God and Father of all,

—Ephesians 4:4-6

This is not a vague ideal. It is a divine blueprint. And we ignore it to our peril.

This Will Take More Than Slogans

Unity cannot be restored by tweeting about love. It will take repentance. It will take fasting, tears, conversations, and courage.

It will require us to relearn how to walk together—even when we disagree. Because division, left unchecked, becomes rebellion. And rebellion against the prayer of Christ is not revival—it is ruin.

We have accepted division as normal. But Christ never did. And if we are to follow Him, we cannot either. Let the rebuilding begin— Rebuilding begins with more than confession—it requires action. What might it look like? Perhaps it starts with pastors praying across denominational lines. With believers from differing traditions serving side-by-side in their city. With small groups gathering not to debate, but to open Scripture together, reasoning in the Spirit as they did in Acts 15—not to win an argument, but to discern the mind of Christ. This is not the unity of compromise. It is the unity of conviction—shared at the foot of the Cross. Not with platforms, but with posture. Not with alliances, but with allegiance. Not with comfort, but with cross-bearing love. Because the Church cannot walk forward if its foundation is broken. And unity—true unity—is the path back.

Becoming Builders, Not Just Believers

A Call to Reconstruct the Body with Obedience, Not Ego

If the walls are cracked, the Watchmen must speak. But words alone are not enough. Sounding the alarm is only the beginning.

When the breach is exposed, the Body doesn't just

need warning— it needs builders. Not builders of brands. Not builders of tribes. Not builders of ministries that reflect personality over purity.

But builders of bridges. Builders of the Body.

Those who remember what the Church is supposed to be. Those who grieve over its fragmentation—not with cynicism, but with resolve.

> "Unless the Lord builds the house, those who build it labor in vain."—Psalm 127:1

The Lord is still building. But many are laboring without Him—constructing visible platforms while the invisible foundations crumble.

Why Builders Must Rise Again

The next generation isn't asking for more polished arguments or better theological branding. They are asking a quieter, more piercing question:

Will the Church still be standing when we arrive?

Not standing in numbers, but in substance. Not standing in reach, but in reverence. Not surviving as an institution, but thriving as a Kingdom witness.

Right now, they see cracks in the walls. They see leaders falling. They see churches splitting. They see more posts about disagreements than about Jesus. And they wonder: *Is this what faithfulness looks like?*

We cannot pass down a fractured inheritance. We cannot model tribalism and expect unity. We cannot defend our camps while pretending to be a Kingdom. If we want to be faithful to the next generation, we must build again.

What Kind of Builders Are We?

Are we building with permanence—or with pride? Are we building systems that preserve ego, or structures that foster humility? Are we constructing walls that insulate us from correction—or bridges that restore fellowship?

We've spent years building brands. Now it's time to build the Body. To do that, we must first acknowledge that the wall is broken.

> *"Every house divided against itself will not stand."*
> *—Matthew 12:25*

This is not a metaphor. It is a spiritual law.

It is Jesus describing what always happens to a divided structure—it collapses. And the longer we ignore the breach, the greater the loss.

The Cost of Rebuilding

True rebuilding will cost us more than energy—it will cost us comfort. It will mean:

- Repenting of prideful positions

- Surrendering tribal allegiances

- Being corrected by brothers we once critiqued

- Shrinking our platforms to make space for the presence of Christ

And it will mean doing all of that together. Because the Church is not a solitary fortress. It is a living temple, built together, stone by stone, on the same Cornerstone.

> *"Let what cannot be shaken remain."*
> *—Hebrews 12:27*

A HOUSE DIVIDED

If we are to endure the shaking, we must rebuild with what will remain: Christ, His Word, and a people unified in Him.

Builders Who Obey, Not Promote

We need builders who are more interested in obedience than reach. Builders who would rather disciple ten with truth than entertain a thousand with novelty. Builders who are not defined by their Twitter bios, but by their burden for the Church. Obedience is not glamorous. It doesn't trend. It doesn't monetize well. But it is what keeps the wall from falling.

When Nehemiah rebuilt the wall around Jerusalem, he didn't do it with fanfare. He did it with resistance. With ridicule. With sword in one hand and brick in the other.

And he did it because the wall mattered— not for its appearance, but for what it protected.

The Church Doesn't Need a Rebrand

There's a growing temptation to treat the Church like a product. To fix its reputation with better messaging. To reclaim credibility through aesthetic updates. To resolve division through clever slogans.

But the Church doesn't need a rebrand. It needs a return. To the Cornerstone. To the Scriptures. To one another. It needs to remember its first love. It needs to confess its compromise. It needs to rebuild—not with worldly metrics, but with Kingdom materials.

We are not marketers. We are laborers in a spiritual field. And the field is not asking for spectacle— it's waiting for fruit.

What We Must Build Toward

We must build toward a Church that:

- Loves truth more than opinion
- Values unity more than agreement
- Submits to Scripture more than systems
- Embraces correction more than applause

We must build toward a Church that is:

- Theologically anchored
- Relationally reconcile
- Spiritually alive
- And eschatologically aware—knowing that Christ is returning for a bride, not a brand

Unity without compromise is possible. But it will never come without cost.

The Final Commission to the Builder

This is not a time to stand on the sidelines. This is a time to rise— with sword in one hand and trowel in the other.

To speak where others are silent. To labor where others have retreated. To contend for truth, not to win— but to restore. Because the Church of Jesus Christ is not beyond repair. But it is in need of builders. And if we do not rebuild now, the next generation may inherit a Church that has learned to exist divided, but has forgotten how to stand unified.

This is the hour. The call has been sounded.

Let the Watchmen speak. Let the builders rise. And let the wall be built again— not in our name, but in His.

A HOUSE DIVIDED

Watchman's Prayer

Lord, expose the cracks we've painted over. Teach us to build—not just react. Let unity rise where pride once stood. Let us become one—not for our sake, but for Yours.
    In Jesus' name,
    Amen.

2

One Gospel, Many Options

Blueprints and Brick Dust

Learning to Discern What Actually Holds the House Together

A wise builder knows that not every line on a blueprint is created equal. Some lines mark load-bearing walls. Others trace plumbing or cabinetry. Still others detail where the windows go or how the paint changes tone. But the foundation—that's another matter. Shift that, and the entire structure groans. Ignore it, and collapse is only a matter of time.

The same is true in theology.

In every generation, the Church drafts its blueprints. Doctrines are outlined. Confessions take shape. Some lines mark what is central: the Trinity—One God in Three Persons; the sovereignty of the Father; the person and work of Jesus Christ; the indwelling power of the Holy Spirit; the Church, salvation, and the coming Kingdom. These are the foundation stones.

Other lines trace helpful but secondary contours—views on spiritual gifts, end-times interpretations, models of governance. They matter. But they are not equal in weight. The wise builder knows the difference.

When Every Line Is Treated Like Load-Bearing

Today's Church often acts as though every line in the blueprint is foundational. Disagreements over baptism methods are treated as breaches of faith. Divergent views on eschatology are labeled as compromise. Secondary doctrines—important, but not salvific—are elevated to salvific status.

And suddenly, the blueprint becomes not a tool for building but a weapon for dividing.

The result? A house groaning under the weight of pride and precisionism. We draw every wall in permanent ink. We issue permits only to those who share our exact floorplan. And when a faithful brother or sister raises a question about a hallway or a side room, we act as though they've jackhammered the foundation.

But not every disagreement is a threat to the structure.

There are doctrines that carry the weight of the house: the identity of Christ, the authority of Scripture, the reality of sin and salvation. And then there are doctrines that shape how the rooms look and function—but are not part of the foundation. Views on the tribulation. The frequency of communion. The mechanics of how the Spirit moves.

When we lose this distinction, we don't strengthen the Church—we fracture it.

A Noisy Construction Site

At times, the modern Church feels less like a unified body and more like a construction site filled with shouting voices. Every worker is convinced their section of the blueprint is central. Every camp insists that their doctrine is the cornerstone. Every platform warns that to disagree is to depart from truth.

The result is dust. Division. A half-built house that frightens away the very people it was meant to shelter. Instead of standing on the clear foundation of Christ and Him crucified, we argue over the color of the bricks. Instead of contending for the faith once delivered to the saints, we spiral into endless contention over interpretive details that do not determine saving faith.

And we wonder why the house doesn't feel like home.

The Gospel Is the Anchor; Everything Else Is the Sail

There is one Gospel. Not several. Not flavors. Not denominational edits or cultural reinterpretations. Just one.

> *"Now I would remind you, brothers, of the gospel I preached to you, which you received, in which you stand, and by which you are being saved..."—1 Corinthians 15:1-2*

Paul did not leave the Church to guess which doctrines matter most. He defines the Gospel as Christ's death, burial, and resurrection, in accordance with the Scriptures. That is the anchor. Without it, we drift. Without it, we sink.

But the Church has also raised sails—and that's not wrong. Traditions. Theological reflections. Historical creeds. These help us catch the wind of wisdom and navigate the world more effectively. They shape our movement. They help us steer.

The problem comes when sails are mistaken for anchors—when personal preferences replace apostolic doctrine. We confuse motion for direction. We lose our center.

It's not the diversity of thought that fractures us— it's the elevation of every thought to ultimate importance. When every hill becomes a hill to die on, we stop building the house and start defending our corners.

This is the heart of what theologians call doctrinal triage—the practice of distinguishing between primary, secondary, and tertiary doctrines. It's not a compromise of conviction. It's an act of wisdom and fidelity.

1. Primary Doctrines: The Anchor of the Faith

These are the non-negotiables. The truths that define Christianity itself:

- The triune nature of God
- The full deity and humanity of Jesus
- The substitutionary death, burial, and resurrection of Christ
- Salvation by grace through faith
- The authority of Scripture
- The bodily return of Christ

Without these, Christianity unravels. These are the truths the early creeds protected, the apostles preached, and the martyrs died to defend. They form the shoreline of orthodoxy. Deny them, and you're not just in rough waters—you're off the map. This is why the early Church formed creeds—not to control minds, but to guard the foundation. The Apostles' Creed and the Nicene Creed did not invent doctrine; they affirmed what Scripture revealed. These confessions have, for centuries, drawn the boundary lines of faithful belief—not as fences of exclusion, but as anchors in turbulent theological waters.

2. Secondary Doctrines: The Sails That Guide the Church

These doctrines matter. They often shape how we gather, worship, and live in community:

- Modes of baptism
- Church government
- Views on communion
- The gifts of the Spirit and their expression

Christians who love the same Gospel may differ here—and that's okay. These convictions may affect where we worship, but they shouldn't affect who we recognize as family.

The problem comes when secondary issues are elevated to salvation tests. That's when a sail becomes mistaken for the anchor—and the ship starts to list.

3. Tertiary Doctrines: The Ropes and Rigging of the Journey

These are issues of interpretation, conscience, and wisdom. They include:

- The timing of Christ's return
- The nature of creation timelines
- Political views

- Personal convictions about alcohol, media, or education

They matter—but they are not central. Yet we must also be vigilant: even tertiary matters—when elevated beyond their place—can begin to influence doctrine. When political identity overshadows spiritual identity, or when lifestyle preferences are canonized as marks of orthodoxy, what begins as conscience can calcify into counterfeit. The problem is not in having convictions. The danger is when those convictions eclipse Christ. They require humility, not hostility. These are places for dialogue, not division.

Disputes That Divide but Shouldn't

Let us name them—the controversies that consume church meetings, launch endless podcasts, and fill comment sections with fire and fury:

- Are tongues for today or only for the apostolic age?
- Did God create the world in six literal days—or over long epochs?
- What's the correct view of the millennium: pre-, post-, or a-millennial?
- Should baptism be by immersion, sprinkling, or reserved for confessing believers only?
- Is communion symbolic or sacramental?
- Is alcohol abstinence a command or a conviction?
- Should worship be led with hymns or guitars, robes or jeans?

These aren't trivial questions. They shape our liturgy, community life, and witness. Faithful believers have wrestled with them for centuries. But this must be said clearly: they are not the Gospel.

The Gospel is not determined by your position on the millennium. No one is justified by their view of baptismal timing. Christ did not die so you could win a doctrinal argument on social media.

He died for sin.

He rose for salvation.

He reigns to unite us to Himself—and to one another.

When we elevate every issue to salvation status, we commit a subtle form of idolatry. We build doctrinal golden calves—constructs shaped by good intentions but worshiped in wrong proportions. And when we demand others bow to them, we fracture the very Body Christ died to make one.

This is not a call to laziness in doctrine. We're called to love God with our minds. But there is a difference between clarity and control—between conviction and condemnation.

When we confuse what's essential with what's important, we stop teaching and start policing. We stop shepherding and start separating. And the Church bleeds because of it.

The Apostles' Pattern: Unity on the Cross, Liberty in the Disputable

The early Church was born into tension—ethnic, theological, cultural. Jews who had waited centuries for the Messiah now sat beside uncircumcised Gentiles. Pharisees turned followers of Jesus worshiped alongside former idolaters. The Body of Christ was diverse from the beginning—and with that diversity came disagreement.

What's remarkable is not that those tensions existed, but how the apostles responded. Their pattern is both simple and profound: unity on the cross, liberty in the disputable.

A HOUSE DIVIDED

This is clearest in Acts 15, at the Jerusalem Council. A sharp debate had erupted: must Gentile believers be circumcised and keep the Law of Moses in order to be saved?

For many Jewish believers, circumcision wasn't cultural—it was covenantal. The Law wasn't optional—it was sacred. But the apostles didn't sidestep the issue. They gathered. They listened. They reasoned together.

Peter stood and reminded them: God had already poured out the Spirit on Gentiles who had done none of these things. No law had been kept. No ritual fulfilled. And yet God had cleansed their hearts by faith.

Then James, the brother of Jesus, offered this judgment:

"It seemed good to the Holy Spirit and to us not to burden you..."

And what followed were not salvation requirements, but pastoral recommendations—guidelines to promote peace.

The apostles made it clear: Circumcision was meaningful to some and offensive to others—but it wasn't the Gospel. Therefore, it wasn't a line to divide over.

Paul carried this spirit into Romans 14, where believers were dividing over sacred days and dietary laws. His counsel? Accept the one whose faith is weak, without quarreling over disputable matters. These weren't meaningless issues—but they weren't Gospel issues. Each believer was to be convinced in their own mind—and neither was to despise the other.

Again in 1 Corinthians 8, Paul addressed food sacrificed to idols. Some knew idols were nothing, so they ate freely. Others abstained, out of conscience. Paul didn't elevate one over the other—he warned them: Knowledge puffs up, but love builds up.

He wasn't asking the Church to flatten all differences. He was calling them to anchor those differences in love. But when Paul did draw a hard line, it wasn't on food or worship style. It was on the Gospel itself.

> *"I delivered to you as of first importance... that Christ died for our sins in accordance with the Scriptures... that He was buried... that He was raised on the third day."—1 Corinthians 15*

This was the center. This was the line that could not move. The apostles did not demand perfect agreement on every issue. But they did create a path to walk together in the midst of disagreement. That path still exists. And it still begins—and ends—with Christ.

When Personal Conviction Becomes Public Law

There's a quiet but corrosive danger in turning personal conviction into public law for the Church. It often begins in sincerity—with a believer seeking to honor God in a specific area of life: in what they eat or drink, how they worship, what boundaries they draw.

But when that believer begins expecting others to adopt their conviction—not as a matter of conscience, but as a standard of righteousness—the trouble begins.

Scripture addresses this tension head-on. Paul, in both Romans and Corinthians, acknowledges that believers will land in different places on disputable matters. Some will abstain out of reverence. Others will participate out of freedom. Both can honor God. Neither should condemn the other.

In Romans 14, Paul urges the strong not to despise the weak, and the weak not to judge the strong. Why? Because each of us will give an account to God. Personal accountability is preserved. Liberty isn't license, but it is real. And conscience matters.

But today, we've often reversed this wisdom. We create church cultures not defined by the Gospel but shaped by collective preference. In the name of conviction, we craft unwritten laws. In the name of purity, we impose burdens Christ never required.

We declare someone unfaithful not for denying Christ, but for worshiping with drums. We question someone's holiness based on attire, liturgy, or leadership style.

This is not contending for the faith. It's mistaking preference for precept. It turns sanctuaries into courtrooms, pulpits into platforms for opinion, and the Gospel into a tool for control.

And often, it masquerades as holiness.

The abstainer may begin to believe they're more devoted. The expressive worshiper, more spiritual. The structured church, more reverent. The spontaneous gathering, more authentic. Slowly, what was a conviction becomes a credential.

But Scripture gives no permission for that shift. Paul didn't condemn those who honored God by abstaining—or those who gave thanks and ate. He condemned those who judged others by their own convictions. He warned against using freedom as a wedge or conscience as a club.

Convictions are sacred. But they are personal—formed under the Lordship of Christ, not enforced by the fellowship.

Yes, the Church must have structure. Yes, some matters are non-negotiable. But we must learn to discern the difference between a Gospel issue and a personal pattern.

Because when we elevate conviction to law, we

place burdens Christ never placed. We exchange grace for performance. And we trade spiritual maturity for spiritual control.

When Gray Becomes a Counterfeit

Not all secondary issues are harmless. While some disagreements arise from sincere study or cultural context, others become something more dangerous. They don't remain theological gray areas. They evolve into platforms—crafted to gather followers, stir controversy, and elevate personalities.

What begins in nuance becomes noise. What starts in curiosity becomes currency.

This is when gray becomes a counterfeit.

The danger isn't in having a unique interpretation. The Church has always needed thinkers who wrestle deeply with Scripture. The problem emerges when minor insights become movements, when speculation becomes identity, and when attention replaces obedience.

A teacher emphasizes obscure numerology. A ministry builds its brand around decoding end-times signs through blood moons or ancient calendars. An online voice claims secret insight missed by others—slowly gathering followers around revelation, not redemption.

And the Body becomes disoriented.

Paul warned Timothy:

"Have nothing to do with foolish, ignorant controversies; you know they breed quarrels."
—2 Timothy 2:23

Elsewhere, he cautions against myths, endless genealogies, and speculative teachings that erode stewardship and promote pride. In Colossians, he warns of hollow philosophy dressed in visions and self-made religion.

The apostles saw it coming.

And the danger today isn't always heresy—it's displacement. The Gospel isn't denied outright. It's just quietly replaced by something more novel. Fascination becomes the fuel. Personal charisma replaces scriptural clarity. And followers begin anchoring themselves to the teacher, not the truth.

It doesn't happen all at once. Over months or years, reinterpretations slip in. Vocabulary remains familiar, but meaning shifts. Definitions of sin, salvation, and Christ's nature are quietly reshaped.

By the time the Word is altered, it's too late. The community is no longer testing by Scripture—they're trusting a personality. Curiosity has replaced conviction. This is how gray becomes a counterfeit—not through loud rebellion, but through slow erosion.

The Gospel, by contrast, is not hidden. It's not encrypted. It doesn't require a secret key or mystical diagram. It is proclaimed. It is plain. And it is enough.

Truth doesn't need to shout. It doesn't need to decorate itself with flair. It simply speaks—and the Spirit convicts.

Error, on the other hand, often insists on a microphone. It markets itself as revelation while recycling confusion.

This is not a call to silence thoughtful teachers. It's a call to accountability. God gives gifts of wisdom and insight—but those gifts must lead to Christ, not center on man. They must deepen our love for Scripture, not replace it with shadows.

When gray becomes a counterfeit, the Church loses clarity—and the world sees a faith that looks more like a conspiracy than a Kingdom.

Let us return to the center.

Let us test the spirits—not just applaud the speaker.

Let us remember: Christ is the mystery revealed, and in Him are hidden all the treasures of wisdom and knowledge.

And He is not for sale.

Unity Demands Discernment, Not Doctrinal Flattery

Let us be clear.

Not every disagreement is disputable. Not every issue belongs in the same category. And not every difference should be handled with polite indifference for the sake of appearing unified.

There is a growing impulse in the modern Church—a movement that seeks unity at any cost. It avoids clarity. It sidesteps theological tension. It substitutes conviction for comfort and trades the foundation of truth for the illusion of peace. But this kind of doctrinal flattery doesn't produce unity. It produces erosion.

The result is a church culture that treats every belief as optional, every interpretation as equal, and every disagreement as something to defer. But this is no better than the dogmatism that fractures over every secondary issue. If doctrinal tribalism is one ditch, then theological ambiguity is the other. And both lead off the road Christ calls us to walk.

The apostles didn't suffer for vague ideas. The martyrs weren't burned for flexible opinions. They died because they refused to deny what was core: the deity of Jesus, the authority of Scripture, the resurrection of the body, salvation by grace through faith.

These truths are not cultural—they're eternal. Not negotiable—but necessary. That's why discernment is not a luxury—it's a mandate. It's not the reflex of arrogance but the fruit of maturity. To discern is to love rightly. To guard what is holy without weaponizing what is secondary.

This does not mean every division is unfaithful. There are moments when separation becomes necessary—not out of preference, but out of fidelity to the Gospel. Paul was uncompromising in Galatians 1:8: if anyone preaches another gospel, "let him be accursed." Apostasy is not disagreement over method—it is departure from the message. And when the foundation is denied, unity must give way to clarity.

We must reclaim the ability to distinguish between categories of belief.

Dogma – the non-negotiables of the Christian faith:

- The Trinity, the full deity and humanity of Christ, the virgin birth, the cross, the resurrection, and the authority of the Word. Deny these, and you're outside the bounds of historic Christianity.

Doctrine – essential for healthy faith and practice, but not for salvation:

- The mode of baptism, spiritual gifts, church governance, or end-times views. Christians may disagree here while still sharing one Spirit and one Lord.

Opinion – personal preferences, cultural expressions, or local practices:

- Service times. Music styles. Dress codes. Sermon length. These shape how we gather—but they don't define whether we belong.
- When these categories are confused, the Church suffers.
- Treat opinion like dogma, and legalism creeps in.

Treat dogma like doctrine, and unity crumbles. Treat everything as gray, and truth disappears altogether.
- Discernment guards against all of it. It teaches us what to hold tightly, what to hold gently, and what to let go. It refuses to exalt tribal language—and it refuses to water down the truth.
- This is not easy work. It takes courage and humility in equal measure—courage to speak when truth is compromised, and humility to listen when others see differently.
- Discernment refuses to turn every disagreement into combat. But it also refuses to let silence masquerade as unity.

We do not honor Christ by flattening all doctrine. We honor Him by holding fast to the truth that saves—while refusing to use theology as a weapon.

This is what Paul modeled. He spoke with fire when the Gospel was at stake. He reasoned with patience when secondary issues arose. He never sacrificed clarity—but he also never fractured the Body over disputable matters.

> *"Make every effort to keep the unity of the Spirit through the bond of peace." – Ephesians 4:3*

Unity isn't something we manufacture. The Spirit gives it. Our job is to protect it—with truth and with love. Unity without discernment isn't unity—it's drift.

Guard the Gospel. Hold the Center. Welcome the Weaker

The Gospel is not fragile. But our handling of it often is.

It has withstood persecution, distortion, neglect, and revival. It has outlasted empires and outshone movements. But when placed in careless or prideful hands, it's misrepresented—shaped to fit agendas or burdened by additions it was never meant to carry.

That's why the Church must be vigilant. Not defensive, but discerning. Not territorial, but truthful. We are not called to fence off the Gospel—but to faithfully guard its boundaries. We don't own the truth. We're stewards—entrusted to preserve it, proclaim it, and pass it on without embellishment or erosion.

To do this, we must hold the sacred tension:

- Build unity without compromising truth
- Welcome brothers and sisters who don't share our timelines or traditions—but who cling to the same Savior
- Draw lines where Scripture draws them—and erase the ones we've added out of pride or fear

We must return to the blueprint.

Not the systems we've stacked on top of it. Not the scaffolding of denominations or traditions. Not the theological frameworks we defend more fiercely than the Gospel itself.

The blueprint is simple. And the apostles left it plain.

"Christ died for our sins. He was buried. He rose again. According to the Scriptures."
—1 Corinthians 15

This is the Gospel of first importance. The cornerstone. The line that cannot move. It's not a metaphor. It's not a myth. It's the historical, theological, and eternal truth: the life, death, and resurrection of Jesus Christ for the salvation of all who believe. From this, we draw every boundary. Around this, we build everything else.

Everything else is brick dust.

Theological brick dust is not evil. It may come from

faithful study. It may offer insight, tradition, or beauty. But it's not the cornerstone. And when we try to rebuild the foundation with it, the structure weakens. We shift weight to what cannot bear it.

That's why we must hold the center. In an age of extremes—where some weaponize every doctrine and others blur every truth—the Church must rediscover the strength of Gospel clarity.

We don't need to be experts in every argument.

We need to be faithful to the one message that saves.

We need to be the people who can listen without surrendering truth—who can speak without crushing the weary. And part of that faithfulness means welcoming the weaker. Paul says in Romans 14:

> *"Accept the one whose faith is weak, without quarreling over disputable matters."*

He's not calling for relativism. He's calling for maturity. To welcome the weaker means making space for those still growing. It means honoring the journey of those whose consciences are still forming. It means protecting them—not by diluting truth, but by leading with love.

It also means recognizing that we may be the weaker one—rigid where Christ gives freedom, or confident in areas where we lack understanding. The Gospel levels us all. It humbles the scholar and lifts the new believer. It leaves no room for boasting—only for worship. And that is the key to unity: not erasing difference, but refusing to divide where God has not.

So we guard the Gospel. We hold the center. And we welcome the weaker.

This is the posture of the Watchman: Eyes on the horizon. Heart grounded in truth. Arms open to the weary.

A HOUSE DIVIDED

Watchman's Prayer

Lord, keep me anchored in Your Gospel. Teach me to hold fast where You have spoken clearly, and to show grace where You have left room for freedom. Let me never elevate my tradition above Your truth. And let Your Church be one— not in flattery, but in faith.

    In Jesus' name,
    Amen.

3

THE RISE OF CELEBRITY CHRISTIANS

From Apostles to Influencers: The Distortion of Spiritual Authority

The Golden Calf Had a Great Following

Division rarely begins with doctrine alone. As we've seen, the fragmentation of the Church often flows downstream from culture—and platform culture has accelerated it. The more we elevate personalities, the more we redefine essentials. Charisma becomes the compass. Influence becomes the standard. And suddenly, the Body is divided—not by creeds, but by crowds. Israel never stopped worshiping.
They just changed the object.
When Moses delayed on the mountain, the people didn't say,

"Let's reject God."

A HOUSE DIVIDED

They said,

"Make us a god we can see. Make us a leader we can rally behind."

So Aaron—pressured and passive—fashioned the golden calf. And they danced. Not in rebellion against worship, but in the redefinition of it. Not atheism, but idolatry dressed in religious enthusiasm.

They still gathered. Still invoked His name. Still offered sacrifices.

But it was no longer Yahweh they followed.

It was an image. A symbol. A substitute—crafted by their hands, crowned by their expectations.

And this is where the echo begins.

The Shift That Didn't Feel Like a Shift

What happened at Sinai wasn't a revolution. It was a slow rotation of loyalty—a shift in spiritual gravity. The people didn't stop being religious. They just replaced the center.

And that's what makes it dangerous.

Counterfeit worship doesn't always feel counterfeit. It carries the same vocabulary. Stirs the same emotions. Gathers the same crowd. But the glory has departed.

So It Is with the Modern Church

We haven't stopped ministry. But we have shifted its center.

We still gather. Still preach. Still lift our hands. Still say His name. But the gravitational pull has changed.

From the glory of Christ to the glow of the stage.

From trembling before the Word to celebrating the one who delivers it with flair.

It's no longer the presence that defines the room—

but the personality. No longer the message that pierces the heart—but the moment that stirs the crowd.

This is not a rejection of Christ. It is the reshaping of His image—tailored to our palates, our branding, our sensibilities.

The Calves We Now Build

The golden calf has not returned in gold.It returns in sneakers and microphones. In charisma without submission. In platform without accountability.In branding that outruns brokenness.

And we—like Israel—don't even recognize it.

Because it still uses the right words. Still raises hands in worship. Still quotes Scripture. Still claims "anointing." But the question is not, Does it look like worship? The question is: Who is being glorified? When the sermon is built around personality... When the lighting is more carefully engineered than the message... When the applause is louder than the altar call...

We are not encountering the Christ who cleanses temples. We are entertaining ourselves before a golden pulpit.

The Platform Can Become an Idol

There is a kind of authority that comes from heaven. And there is another that comes from algorithm.

One is forged in the fire of obedience. The other is curated, filtered, and optimized for engagement.

In an age flooded with content, the Church has not stayed distinct. We've been tempted to compete with influencers rather than be formed by intercession. We measure impact by reach, not by reverence. We confuse attention for anointing. We reward gifting over fruit.

But when the platform becomes the goal, the Gospel becomes a prop. The message becomes a means to build me. The pulpit becomes a stage. The sheep become spectators. And the shepherd becomes a performer.

Paul Saw It Coming

> *"If someone comes and proclaims another Jesus... or a different gospel... you put up with it readily enough."*—2 Corinthians 11:4

Paul warned of a Church that would tolerate distortion—not because the message was compelling, but because the messenger was impressive.

He foresaw a day when a different Jesus, a different spirit, and a different gospel would be welcomed simply because they arrived in polished packaging.

And that day is now.

The Danger Is Subtle

Not all false teaching is blatant. Some is Scripture-scented. Some wears the garments of truth while centering the self.

The danger in modern platforms is not always in heresy. It's in truth delivered without holiness. It's in eloquence unaccompanied by obedience. It's in bold proclamation without broken posture.

Not every false teacher lies about Jesus. Some just replace Him with themselves—center stage, center screen, center of attention. They may quote the Word. They may preach the cross. But when the message ends, it is not the crucified Christ who remains—it is their charisma.

Celebrity Christianity Is Structural Failure

Celebrity Christianity is not merely moral failure. It is structural failure.

It's the slow erosion of sacred ecosystems—spaces meant to exalt Christ, now redesigned to elevate personalities.

Churches don't fall into this all at once. They slide.

From discipleship to fanbase. From pastor to brand. From pulpit to performance. From truth-telling to trend-tracking.

At first, no one notices. The sermons still name Jesus. The songs still say "Holy Spirit." The lighting still shifts at the right cue.

But over time, something holy is replaced by something hollow. Not because of what's said— but because of who's being centered.

From Apostles to Influencers

We have watched the shift. What began with a burden to reach the lost has slowly morphed into a mechanism to expand personal brands.

Megachurch empires now run on marketing pipelines. Preachers become podcasters. Podcasters become CEOs. Worship leaders headline global tours with merch tables beside the altar.

The call to go and make disciples has been reshaped into build and grow your audience.

And with the rise— we have seen the fall.

The Trail of Collapse

A HOUSE DIVIDED

We've seen the headlines. The scandals. The resignations. The carefully crafted "rest and reflection" posts. But behind the fall is a system that rewarded image over integrity.

- Moral failures buried under loyalty oaths and legal shields
- Abuse minimized by PR teams
- Doctrine diluted for "relevance"
- Giving manipulated to sustain unsustainable lifestyles

These are not isolated incidents. They are signs of scaffolding we built— and now blame the wind for knocking down.

We Built This

We did not inherit this structure from the apostles. We assembled it— brick by branded brick.

We traded apostolic grit for production gloss. We turned shepherds into content curators. We built churches like corporations, hired based on personality, measured success by metrics, and crowned charisma over character.

And now, when it all collapses, we act surprised. We blame "culture." But the scaffolding was ours.

This is not just failure. It is spiritual malpractice.

The Metrics We Worship

Influence is not evil. But influence without formation is dangerous.

Let it be said: gifting is not the enemy. The Church has always been blessed by faithful communicators, anointed musicians, and wise leaders. Their reach is not a liability—unless it outruns their surrender. When gifting is stewarded through humility, and when platforms serve rather than seduce, fruit abounds. The problem is never the gift—it is when the gift replaces the Giver.

And right now, our metrics look nothing like Christ's:

- Growth = God's favor
- Platform = anointing
- Stage presence = authority
- Engagement = fruit

We quote Jesus but follow the algorithm. We say

"Thy Kingdom come,"

but we build sanctuaries stamped with our names. This is not persecution. This is pride. And pride always collapses.

The Algorithm as Disciple-Maker

Social media didn't invent this drift. But it amplified it—at scale.

- Quiet pastors are buried by noise
- Sermons are crafted for clips, not conviction
- Churches are shaped by what performs on reels
- Repentance is replaced by next-event promotions

The algorithm rewards novelty. It rewards outrage. It rewards charisma.

It does not reward holiness.

And even the faithful feel the pressure: To perform. To produce. To be seen. But faithfulness doesn't trend. And it never had to.

The Influence Trap

A HOUSE DIVIDED

Even good men fall for it. Even sincere women bend toward it.

Not out of rebellion— but out of slow redefinition.

What begins in mission ends in marketing.

No one sets out to build a ministry that collapses. But if we construct with visibility and ignore depth— collapse is guaranteed.

We were called to make disciples. But we've created fanbases.

We made the Gospel viral— but lost its offense. We made pastors accessible— but never accountable. We monetized the platform— but abandoned the altar.

Paul, the Anti-Celebrity Apostle

Paul had influence. But he never sought fans. He wasn't building a tribe. He wasn't branding a movement. He wasn't optimizing sermons for engagement. He was pouring out his life so that Christ would be formed in others. And when the Corinthians began dividing along human lines—

> "I follow Paul... Apollos... Cephas..."

—he asked the question that slices through every cult of personality:

> "Was Paul crucified for you?"
> —1 Corinthians 1:13

That is the cry of a man unwilling to share Christ's glory.

Rival Fanbases Then

The Corinthians didn't deny Christ. They just preferred

their favorite spokesperson. As if truth needed packaging. As if Jesus needed branding.

We do the same today. We don't say,

> "I follow Christ."

We say,

> "I follow [insert preacher, stream, influencer]."

We claim to be Gospel-centered— but our loyalty often says otherwise.

Paul didn't just reject the praise. He dismantled the system.

> "We preach Christ crucified."

Not Paul. Not Apollos. Not Peter. Christ.

Paul's Leadership Model

In 1 Corinthians 3, Paul gets explicit:

> "So neither he who plants nor he who waters is anything, but only God who gives the growth."
> —1 Corinthians 3:7

That one line destroys modern ministry pride.

Paul insists: I am not the source. Apollos is not the source. Only God brings growth.

Paul wasn't a CEO. He wasn't a guru. He was a laborer—planting, sweating, weeping in the dirt while God caused the seed to break open and grow. He did not want followers. He wanted a faithful Church.

Paul's Posture: Weakness, Not Stagecraft

When Paul arrived in Corinth, he didn't walk in with entourage and confidence.

He said:

> "I came to you in weakness and in fear and much trembling."
> —1 Corinthians 2:3

Not exactly the bio of a headlining speaker.

He was scarred. Unimpressive. Often rejected. He made tents to survive. He defended his apostleship from critics. He bled more than he was believed.

And yet— he turned the world upside down.

Because his power didn't come from presence. It came from brokenness.

What Made Paul Dangerous

It wasn't polish. It was purity.

He had been blinded by glory—then sent to carry it with scars. He could not be bought. He would not water down the Gospel. He would not bend for applause.

Paul was dangerous to darkness because he feared God more than failure. Because he would rather die in chains than preach a softer Christ.

That's apostolic leadership.

The Model We've Forsaken

We claim to want

> "New Testament Christianity."

But do we want Paul's posture?

- Weakness instead of charisma?
- Obscurity instead of growth?
- Scars instead of spotlights?

We say we follow the same Gospel. But we often follow a different model. Paul didn't trend. He died daily. And in that dying— he showed us how to live.

Fruit Over Following

In today's Church, success is often unspoken—but universally recognized:

- How many followers do they have?
- How large is their church?
- How polished are their sermons?
- How strong is their brand presence?

But Jesus never applauded follower counts. He never praised production value. He never equated impact with visibility.

He said one thing:

"You will recognize them by their fruits."
—Matthew 7:16

Not by their reels. Not by their stagecraft. By their fruit.

What Heaven Actually Measures

True spiritual leadership isn't measured by:

- Attendance
- Aesthetic
- Eloquence

- Influence

It is measured by:

- Humility beneath the Word
- Consistency in hidden obedience
- Repentance when wrong
- Sacrificial love that bleeds quietly
- Character that endures

Fruit doesn't grow in the spotlight. It grows in the secret place— watered by repentance, pruned by correction, and nourished by surrender.

The Weight of the Pulpit

> *"Not many of you should become teachers,"*

James warns,

> *"for you know that we who teach will be judged with greater strictness."—James 3:1*

But today?
We give microphones to the eloquent—before we test their foundation. We celebrate the gifted—before we examine the fruit. We reward charisma—and neglect cruciform living. We platform speed over sanctification. And then act surprised when things collapse.

What We've Accidentally Built

We've built:

- Ministries that can't be questioned

- Leaders who can't be corrected
- Structures that protect charisma but not integrity
- Cultures that prize innovation more than intercession

We planted for applause —and expected holiness to grow. But if the root is ego, the fruit will eventually rot.

Recognizing Rotten Fruit

Not all false teachers distort doctrine. Some distort posture.
They preach the cross— but center themselves.
They say all the right things— but the Spirit is grieved.

Watch for:

- Defensiveness under scrutiny
- Absence of accountability
- Disciples who mimic pride, not Christ
- Obsession with numbers, not names
- Quick growth, no depth

These aren't flukes. They're fruit.

Slow Fruit Is Still Fruit

Paul warned Timothy:

> *"Do not be hasty in the laying on of hands."*
> *—1 Timothy 5:22*

Spiritual fruit takes time.
Before microphones, observe how a life bends under pressure. Before celebration, watch how a leader loves when no one is looking.

A HOUSE DIVIDED

Paul told Titus to find leaders who were (Titus 1:6-9):

- Above reproach
- Sober-minded
- Self-controlled
- Hospitable
- Sound in doctrine

Not flashy. Not viral. Holy.

Let Us Not Be Fooled

A man can trend for years and still be barren before God. A woman can speak eloquently but bear no fruit that remains.

Paul himself said:

> "I discipline my body... lest after preaching to others I myself should be disqualified."
> —1 Corinthians 9:27

That's the fear of the Lord. That's what we've lost.

What We Must Recover

We must raise the standard:

- Not of polish, but purity
- Not of eloquence, but endurance
- Not of reach, but reverence

Look for:

- Teachers who repent quickly
- Leaders who deflect praise

- Shepherds who bleed for the sheep
- Disciples who study in silence and obey in secret

Reflection: What Heaven Will Applaud

The platform will disappear. The stage will fall. The followers will fade.

But Christ will still ask:

Did you love the truth? Did you guard the Gospel? Did you lay down your life?

He's not impressed by fame. He's searching for fruit.

Restore the Authority of the Word, Not the Stage

The solution is not to retreat from visibility. The Church is called to be seen— to be light in darkness, a city on a hill. But visibility must never replace authority. And the only true authority is the Word of God.

Stagecraft Is Not Shepherding

When stage presence becomes the goal, we build churches that impress men but do not tremble before God.

We've learned to:

- Script moments
- Engineer emotions
- Optimize engagement

But none of these substitute for power. Because God does not move through performance— He moves through the Word.

A HOUSE DIVIDED

We've Lost Our Center

The modern pulpit often begins with:

- A joke
- A story
- A set of branded slides

Then the Word is added— not as foundation, but as a garnish.

The result?

- Sermons that mention Scripture but do not submit to it
- Leaders who inspire but do not rightly divide
- Churches that grow in size but shrink in conviction

The Word Must Rule Again

The Bible is not a prop. It is not a backdrop. It is not seasoning for a message already decided in the heart of man.

It is:

- Fire
- Sword
- Seed
- Final authority

It convicts. It sanctifies. It births the fear of the Lord.

And when it is central—truly central—three things happen:

1. Preaching slows down – not to bore, but to cut precisely
2. Leaders bow low – not to culture, but to command
3. The Church matures – not around personality, but around Christ

What Happens When the Stage Replaces the Word

When the Word is no longer the center, the symptoms emerge:

- Sermons become motivational monologues
- Conviction gives way to comfort
- Church becomes a weekly event, not a covenant Body
- People grow attached to personalities, not to Christ

And perhaps worst of all— the voice of Christ is drowned out by the voice of man.

We Must Return to Reverence

God is not impressed by lights, logos, or livestreams. He is drawn to reverence.

> *"This is the one to whom I will look: he who is humble and contrite in spirit and trembles at My word."*
> —Isaiah 66:2

That's the posture He honors. Not the trending preacher. Not the well-packaged sermon.
The trembling servant.

A HOUSE DIVIDED

Rebuild the Pulpit

The pulpit is not a stage. It is a sacred place.
We must stop asking:

> *"Did the room respond?"*
> *"Was the message engaging?"*
> *"Did it trend?"*

And start asking:

> *"Was the Word rightly handled?"*
> *"Was Christ lifted high?"*
> *"Did the Spirit convict and stir repentance?"*

The Church doesn't need more energy. It needs more exegesis.

Reflection: Let the Word Speak Again

The Word is not weak. It doesn't need amplification— it needs reverence. It doesn't need a brand—it needs obedience. The Church will not rise on strategies. It will rise on Scripture.

Let the Word speak again. Let it cut again. Let it thunder again— not through human brilliance, but through broken vessels who know that God still speaks through what He has already spoken.

Fame Fades. Servanthood Remains.

Fame is fleeting. Trends change. The algorithm forgets. The crowd that cheers today may cancel tomorrow. But there is a posture that outlasts applause: the posture of a servant.

The World Celebrates Visibility

It builds statues for popularity. It monetizes charisma. It elevates those who impress. But the Kingdom honors something else:

- Obedience in obscurity
- Faithfulness when no one sees
- Sacrifice without recognition

Because heaven's metrics are not like man's.

A Generation Called to the Back Row

We do not need another wave of Christian influencers. We need a generation that:

- Prepares in the secret place
- Trembles before opening the Word
- Values faithfulness over fame
- Seeks Jesus more than an audience

This is the generation the Spirit is forming— quiet, holy, unseen by man, but known in heaven.

God Begins in Obscurity

Moses was called from the wilderness. David was found with sheep. Elijah heard God in silence. John the Baptist came from the desert. Even Jesus spent thirty years in obscurity before three years of ministry.
Why?
Because obscurity purifies motives.
This is not a call to flee responsibility. Hiddenness is not cowardice—it is consecration. God does not hide

A HOUSE DIVIDED

His servants to withhold them, but to refine them. Before leadership is exercised publicly, it must be sanctified privately. Obscurity does not diminish calling; it deepens it—so that when the time comes to speak, it is Christ who is heard.

It breaks the need to be seen. It forms depth, not just reach.

Christ Modeled the Hidden Path

- He withdrew from the crowd.
- He silenced the healed.
- He rebuked self-promotion.
- He entered Jerusalem not on a warhorse, but on a donkey.
- He washed feet when He could have summoned angels.

"Whoever would be great among you must be your servant."
—Matthew 20:26

This is the Kingdom way. Downward. Hidden. Holy.

Fame Cannot Hold You

Fame is fragile:

- Given quickly
- Lost suddenly
- Unable to sustain the weight of glory

It tempts. It inflates. It deceives. And when it

crumbles, so does the ministry built on it. But servanthood remains.

What Christ Will Remember

When the lights dim, when the account slows, when the sermon clip is forgotten...
What will heaven recall?

- The shepherd who fed a small flock with trembling
- The intercessor who prayed through the night
- The missionary no one knew
- The parent who wept and discipled in secret
- The pastor who never trended, but stood faithful

These are not footnotes in the Kingdom. They are heroes.

The Signature of Christ

He did not chase applause. He bore a cross. He did not rise through branding. He descended into death. His badge of honor? A towel. A crown of thorns. A scarred body. And He calls us to walk the same way.

Let Servanthood Remain

When the lights fade, let your posture remain bowed. When your name is forgotten, let your faith still be found. Because the platform is not the prize. Christ is. And if all that remains is a life poured out at His feet—that is enough.

The Watchman's Benediction: Quiet Again

A HOUSE DIVIDED

It's quiet now. The lights are off. The applause has faded. And no one is watching.

This is where truth waits.

Not in the echo of the crowd, but in the silence that reveals who we really are. Not in what we built publicly, but in what we bowed to privately.

The stage never sanctified the soul. Only presence does. And presence begins with stillness, with surrender, with silence.

Who Are We Without the Applause?

When the green room is empty... When the metrics stall... When the algorithm forgets your name...

Who are we?

This is the question the Watchman must answer. Because before revival comes in power, it comes in obscurity.

Back to the wall. Back to the wilderness. Back to the altar. Back to the quiet.

We've Left the Sacred for the Spectacle

The tabernacle did not shimmer with spotlights. It burned with holy fire.

- Moses entered to fall down, not perform.
- Priests offered sacrifice with blood on their hands, not polish on their image.
- Prophets wept.
- Apostles planted churches—and died for them.

We've replaced glory with glow. Holiness with hype. But God still comes—Not in the curated moment, but in the contrite heart.

The Remnant Will Not Chase Applause

There is a remnant rising. They do not need branding. They do not seek platforms.
They are:

- Watchmen who pray more than they post
- Intercessors who carry burdens in secret
- Shepherds who tremble at the Word
- Saints who are unshaken by fame because they never sought it

They labor where no camera rolls. They kneel when no one claps. They bleed for the Church—not to trend, but to be faithful.

A Posture for the Last Days

The last days will not be sustained by celebrity. They will be sustained by consecration.
Not the most followed— but the most rooted.

- Rooted in truth
- Rooted in fear of the Lord
- Rooted in calling too holy to brand

If Christ is returning for a Bride without spot or wrinkle, He is not coming for a Church intoxicated by applause— but one washed in the Word, and clothed in humility.

Lay It All Down

If you have a platform, use it. But make sure Christ is the one speaking. If you've been called into hiddenness, don't resist it. There is no safer place than where only heaven

A HOUSE DIVIDED

sees. Let the altar be more precious than the audience. Let the Word be more treasured than the reaction. Let the Cross be lifted higher than your own name.

What the Watchman Knows

The Watchman does not despise the noise—but he sees through it.

He knows Christ's glory is not revealed through volume, but through obedience. He knows revival will not come on a branded schedule— but when the people return to the altar with clean hands and contrite hearts.

His cry is simple:

Leave the stage. Return to the altar. And wait for fire.

The Benediction of the Quiet

So we end not in anger. Not in despair. But in clarity. Let the stage dim. Let the spotlight pass. Let the microphone rest. And let Christ be seen again— not in the spotlight, but in the servant who kneels. Because when all the noise falls away, only one voice remains:

> *"This is My beloved Son—hear Him."*
> *—Luke 9:35*

Let that voice be enough. Let it shape a generation. Let it rebuild the pulpit. Let it define the Church. And may the next movement of God rise not from a microphone— but from an altar where everything else was laid down.

Watchman's Prayer:

Lord, strip us of the need to be seen. Rescue the Church from the seduction of platform and applause. Raise up shepherds who tremble before Your Word. Let us follow the towel, not the spotlight. Let us bear crosses, not build brands.

In Jesus' name,
Amen.

4

The Battle For Biblical Interpretation

Sola Scriptura vs Denominational Filters: Can We Read The Bible

The Stained Glass Lens

Scripture was meant to be a window. Clear. Illuminating. Direct. A way to see through the noise of this world into the mind of God. Not a riddle. Not a fog. Not an enigma. A revelation.

> "The entrance of thy words giveth light; it giveth understanding unto the simple."—Psalm 119:130

This was the gift. The promise. The intent. But somewhere along the line, we turned that window into stained glass.

Beautiful, But Broken

Stained glass is reverent. It is crafted with care. It tells stories with beauty. But it does something dangerous: it distorts the light.

It fractures it into colors. It separates it into panels. It dazzles more than it illuminates. Each pane is shaped by tradition. Each hue tinted by interpretation. Each section a mosaic of theological assumptions, historical movements, and denominational inheritance.

What was once a clear pane is now a collage—precious, but complicated. Honored, but no longer plain. Holy, but now hidden behind layers.

The light still shines. But not as it once did. Not straight. Not unfiltered. Now, before it reaches the heart, it is passed through systems, commentaries, creeds, and camps.

What Was Once Plain Is Now Protected

In the early Church, the Word of God was proclaimed openly, copied passionately, and read by fishermen, widows, and jailers.

It confronted kings and comforted children. It spoke plainly. It healed quickly.

But over time, it became less accessible.

- Protected by language barriers
- Guarded by clerical classes
- Encased in systems only the trained could decipher

We do not mean to dishonor church history or the faithful efforts of those who came before. But somewhere along the way, the window became sacred for its frame, not for its view.

We admired the craft more than the content. We

passed on doctrine more than discipleship. We taught people what to think before they ever learned how to read the Word for themselves.

The Word That Was Meant to Unite Has Become a Battlefield

The Word was never meant to be a club. It was meant to be a compass. It was never meant to divide believers over terms and tribes. It was meant to unify the Church under truth.

But today?

We argue over Greek tenses. We split churches over phrases. We treat metaphors like minefields and parables like puzzles. And while we dissect, we no longer digest.

Doctrine matters. Deep study matters. But when theological precision becomes a barricade, rather than a bridge, we've lost the way.

We no longer ask,

"What does God say?"

We ask,

"What does my denomination say about what God says?"

From Lamp to Labyrinth

What was once a lamp to the feet has become, for many, a labyrinth. A maze of positions and traditions and controversies.

A new believer opens their Bible, and within moments they are told:

"Be careful—don't read that like a Charismatic."
"Watch out—this passage is used by Arminians."
"This only makes sense if you hold to Covenant Theology."

A HOUSE DIVIDED

> *"This story is allegorical—unless you're dispensational."*
> *"Only read this book with this commentary beside you."*

They were looking for light. They found a map filled with booby-traps.

And the result?

They stop reading.

Not because they don't love the Word, but because they've been taught that without the right lens, they can't understand it anyway.

We Approach with Bias, Not Wonder

The problem is not simply in the systems. It's in the assumptions we bring when we open the Book.

We read not to be transformed—but to be confirmed. We read not to listen—but to defend. We come to the Scriptures with a preferred outcome—and we make sure the text gets us there.

- We highlight verses that fit our camp.
- We sideline those that complicate our narrative.
- We quote the scholars that agree with us.
- We dismiss the ones that don't.

We don't gaze through the window anymore. We project onto it.

What We've Lost

We've lost the childlike awe. The first-love hunger. The sense that God is speaking, not just scholars.

We've trained a generation to be disciples of theological systems—but not disciples of the voice of the Shepherd.

And yet, Scripture still stands. Still speaks. Still cuts. Still heals.

> *"Is not my word like fire, declares the Lord, and like a hammer that breaks the rock in pieces?"*
> —Jeremiah 23:29

The fire still burns. The hammer still strikes. But we must learn to open the window again—without filters.

The Window Still Stands

Despite our traditions, despite our tribes, despite our theological walls— the Word remains.

The clarity is still there. The Spirit still guides. The truth is still strong enough to pierce without needing our commentary.

What we need is not new lenses, but renewed eyes. Eyes that come to the Word to be changed, not just to be right.

We must open the Bible like it's bread, not blueprint. Like it's living, not literary. Like it's sacred, not strategic.

Reflection: Look Again

The window still stands. But few gaze through it without already expecting to see something familiar.

What would happen if we came with no agenda? No doctrinal checklist. No tribal loyalty.

What if we simply asked,

> *"Lord, show me Yourself in Your Word"*?

Not to support my framework. Not to verify my theology. But to see You. Know You. Obey You. The stained glass can be beautiful. But it was never meant to replace the view. Let the light shine through again— unfiltered. undistorted. and clear.

Sola Scriptura Is Not Solo Scriptura

At the heart of the Reformation stood a thunderous rally cry: Sola Scriptura — Scripture alone.

It was not a cry of isolation, but of liberation. Not a rejection of history, but a return to divine authority. Not the beginning of chaos, but the recovery of order.

The Church had drifted. Rome had crowned tradition as king. Priests mediated access. Papal decrees competed with revelation. Ordinary believers—hungry for God—were told to come only by way of the institution. But the Reformers stood firm: The final word belongs to the Word of God.

> *"All Scripture is given by inspiration of God, and is profitable for doctrine, for reproof, for correction, for instruction in righteousness."—2 Timothy 3:16*

Scripture is not supplementary. It is supreme. It is not commentary on another truth—it is the truth. It interprets the Church; the Church does not interpret it. It binds the conscience; no council may override it. But today, the doctrine of Sola Scriptura has been misused. For some, it no longer means Scripture over tradition. It means Scripture without accountability.

We now see the rise of Solo Scriptura:

> *"I don't need teachers."*
> *"I don't need context."*
> *"I don't need history."*
> *"I don't need community."*

This is not liberty. It is theological anarchy. The Bible becomes a private playground—where every believer builds their own tower of doctrine.

Solo Scriptura places self above Scripture—and calls it faith. It is the equal and opposite error of Rome's overreach. One exalts institution. The other exalts individualism. And both remove the Word from its rightful throne.

True Sola Scriptura calls us to:

- Submit to the Word, not our tribe.
- Test tradition, not discard it.
- Learn from teachers, not idolize them.
- Read in community, but let Scripture rule.

Sola Scriptura is not a slogan. It is a posture. It kneels under the Word, trembles at its voice, and submits every insight, impression, and interpretation to the unchanging text.

What Sola Scriptura Truly Means

We say we're

"biblically based."

We quote Scripture in sermons and songs. We place Sola Scriptura on banners and church signs. But do we understand what it means?

At its core:

- The Bible alone is divinely inspired and without error.
- It is the final and highest authority over every teaching, tradition, and spiritual experience.

A HOUSE DIVIDED

What Sola Scriptura affirms:

- Scripture is God-breathed, not man-crafted (2 Timothy 3:16).
- Its meaning is clear to the humble, not hidden for the elite.
- Doctrine is formed by what God has said—not what we feel, inherit, or assume.
- Scripture interprets Scripture. Not systems. Not sentiments.

You don't need Greek to meet Christ. You don't need a degree to understand the Gospel. The truth is revealed to fishermen and farmers, not just theologians.

> "The unfolding of Your words gives light; it gives understanding to the simple."—Psalm 119:130

What Sola Scriptura does not mean:

- That we reject the role of teachers. (Ephesians 4 makes them essential.)
- That tradition has no value. (We honor creeds—but test them.)
- That theology froze in the 1500s. (We build on the Reformers—we don't canonize them.)
- That private revelation replaces the Word. (God may speak—but never contradicts Himself.)

Sola Scriptura is not

> "Bible only"

in isolation. It is Bible supreme over all else. And

it demands that we read the Word with humility, hunger, and submission—not as a weapon to wield, but a voice to obey.

When Systems Replace Scripture

Let us name the challenge plainly: Many believers today no longer read the Bible directly. They read it through a system. Not always intentionally. Not always maliciously. But consistently.

The lens goes on before the Book is opened. And once that lens is in place, we no longer hear what God has said—we start reinforcing what man has assumed.

The Systems We Love

Calvinism vs. Arminianism. Dispensationalism vs. Covenant Theology. Reformed vs. Charismatic. Literal vs. Allegorical interpretation.

These systems form our camps. They shape our sermons. They guide our discipleship. They define what we believe is "faithful" interpretation.

But here is the key: These systems are not evil. Many were forged in fires of persecution and revival. They were built by men and women of great faith and great intellect—seeking to honor God and preserve doctrinal clarity. They help us process complexity, guard against heresy, and connect the grand story of Scripture.

When rightly constructed—built from the whole counsel of Scripture rather than imposed upon it—systematic theology can help us see the patterns, covenants, and coherence of God's Word more clearly. It's not the presence of a system that's dangerous—it's when the system becomes the master, and Scripture its servant.

But even good systems can become dangerous.

A HOUSE DIVIDED

When Tools Become Filters

The problem is not that we have systems. The problem is when those systems become filters instead of tools. A tool serves the builder. A filter serves the narrative.

And when we begin to see everything through our chosen lens, the Scriptures no longer shape our theology. They simply reinforce it. We come to the text not to listen—but to confirm.

Slowly, subtly, the system replaces Scripture as our final authority.

What This Looks Like in Practice

A passage on election becomes a prooftext for predestination—not a moment of praise. Romans 9 becomes a battleground, not a doxology.

A healing in the Gospels becomes a debate over cessationism, rather than an encounter with the compassion of Christ.

A parable is squeezed until it fits a system. The Sermon on the Mount is softened to match our eschatology. The warnings of Hebrews are dulled to protect our soteriology.

The Bible is no longer read for what it says. It is co-opted to defend what we already believe.

The Apostles Didn't Walk in Systems

Peter wasn't a Calvinist. Paul wasn't a dispensationalist. John wasn't a charismatic—or a cessationist.

They didn't divide the Scriptures into reformed, covenantal, or allegorical compartments. They simply walked with Jesus.

They interpreted the Old Testament through the lens

of Christ, not through theological camps. They read with awe, not just alignment. They taught from conviction, not consensus. Their authority came not from systematizing the truth, but from seeing the Truth made flesh.

Interpretation as Identity

And yet, here we are: Where our systems have become not just tools, but badges. Labels. Tribes.
We no longer ask,

> *"What does the Word say?"*

We ask,

> *"What does my camp say about this?"*

Correction now feels like betrayal. Disagreement becomes division. Echo chambers form. Group consensus replaces personal study.
We don't invite others into discussion—we guard the perimeter. We don't read to learn—we read to defend.
The Spirit no longer leads. Groupthink does.

Paul Saw This Coming

This is not a modern issue. It's an ancient one.

> *"Each one of you says, 'I follow Paul,' or 'I follow Apollos,' or 'I follow Cephas,' or 'I follow Christ.' Is Christ divided?"—1 Corinthians 1:12–13*

Paul wasn't against teachers. He was against tribalism masquerading as sound doctrine. He reminded the Church: You were not baptized in the name of Paul. You were baptized into Christ.

What We Lose

Tribal theology leads to:

- Lost humility – mocking others who love the same Lord but differ in emphasis.
- Lost hunger – reading only for ammunition, not transformation.
- Lost unity – measuring fellowship by confessions, not by the cross.
- Lost witness – a world that sees factions instead of faith.

And worst of all: We lose the power of Scripture to transform us—because we no longer let it speak freely. We've already decided what it's allowed to say.

From Identity Back to Submission

The solution is not to abandon doctrine. The solution is to abandon pride.

Your identity is not your denomination. Not your theology. Not your teacher. Not your system. Your identity is this:

> "I have been crucified with Christ. It is no longer I who live, but Christ who lives in me..."
> —Galatians 2:20

When that becomes your center again, everything else realigns:

- Curiosity replaces defensiveness.
- Worship replaces warfare.
- Submission replaces identity.

The Watchman's Posture

The Watchman does not sound the alarm to defend a tribe. He sounds it to protect the truth. He listens for the Shepherd's voice—not the applause of his camp. He tests everything—not from suspicion, but from trembling.

His loyalty is not to a stream, a scholar, or a system. It is to the Word. The cross. The Son. And so must ours be.

Reflection: Let Scripture Shape You Again

If interpretation has become your identity, lay it down. Lay down the fear of being wrong. Lay down the pride of being precise. Lay down the loyalty that looks more like branding than belief.

Return to the Word—not as a system to defend, but as a fire to be refined by. Christ is not divided. And truth cannot be contained in a tribe. Let the Word shape you again. Let it correct you again. Let it change what you thought you knew. Because in the end, we are not called to be interpreters of our system—We are called to be disciples of His voice.

The Gospel Is Clearer Than We Pretend

We must ask honestly: Have we made the Bible harder than God intended?

Not shallow. Not simplistic. But clear. And not clear to the clever— Clear to the humble. To the hungry. To the ones who still read expecting to hear.

God did not breathe out His Word for the academy. He gave it to shepherds and sinners, mothers and martyrs. To fishermen, tentmakers, and exiles.

For centuries, the Church heard clearly: Jesus is

Lord. Sin is real. Salvation is by grace through faith. The cross is enough.

They didn't parse Greek declensions or systematize election. They wept over Psalms. They whispered Isaiah 53 at funerals. They taught their children the Ten Commandments. They clung to Romans while in chains. They didn't dissect Revelation—they stood on its promises.

They read with tears, not tools. And God met them there.

> *"The unfolding of your words gives light; it gives understanding to the simple."*—Psalm 119:130

This is not a poetic flourish. It's a promise.

The Spirit Still Meets the Hungry

The Holy Spirit was not poured out only for preachers and professors. He is the Interpreter of the submitted soul. He teaches the child and the elder. He reveals to the meek what remains hidden from the proud.

Jesus said,

> *"My sheep hear my voice."*

Not,

> *"My scholars decipher my riddles."*

The Spirit does not bypass truth—He applies it. Not just to the intellect—but to the heart. Not just for knowledge—but for transformation.

We Must Recover First-Love Reading

We need to read the Bible again like it's alive.

Not to perform. Not to argue. But to worship. To listen.

What does that look like?

- Not rejecting scholarship, but refusing to be ruled by it
- Not isolating from community, but taking personal responsibility
- Not defending our system, but submitting it to the text

First-love reading happens when awe outweighs analysis. When encounter outruns commentary. When we stop trying to impress others with our insights— and start longing to meet the One who speaks.

The Word Was Meant to Be Bread, Not a Puzzle

We've turned the Bible into a puzzle. A code. A maze of hidden symbols decipherable only by the initiated. But God described His Word differently:

- Bread for the hungry
- Light for the lost
- Fire for the cold
- Water for the thirsty
- Seed for the soil
- Sword for the deceived

None of these require credentials. They require hunger. Do you need wisdom? Read. Do you need courage? Read. Do you need healing? Read. Read slowly. Read with trembling. Read as if your soul depends on it—because it does.

Let the Word Reintroduce Itself

A HOUSE DIVIDED

Familiarity is sometimes the enemy of clarity. We skim what we think we already know. We quote verses we haven't heard in years.

But what if God wants to show you something new through what is old?

Read John 3:16 like it's not a slogan but a revelation. Read Acts 2 like the Spirit still descends. Read Isaiah 53 as if Christ fulfilled it yesterday. Read Revelation not to map the end—but to worship the King.

The Gospel is not hidden. We just forgot how to look.

Clarity Is Found in Christ, Not Complexity

We mistake depth for confusion. But the Gospel is deep because it's clear.

Jesus is the center. He is the through-line of every story, symbol, psalm, and promise. And when He takes His rightful place, The Bible burns again.

> *"Did not our hearts burn within us... while he opened to us the Scriptures?"—Luke 24:32*

Let it burn again.

Reflection: Return to the Simplicity That Saves

The Gospel is not complicated. We are.

Our systems are. Our tribal allegiances are. Our filters are.

But the Word? It speaks. To the quiet. To the broken. To the hungry.

So stop pretending the Gospel is too hard to understand. Open the Book. And let it open you.

Contextual. Careful. Christ-Centered.

Interpretation is not innovation. It is not performance. It is not a platform.

Interpretation is stewardship. You are handling the voice of God. And you will give account.

As Watchmen, we do not come to the Word to be original. We come to be faithful. To guard what is written. To speak what God has already said— With reverence. With clarity. Without compromise.

There is a triad that keeps us grounded: Contextual. Careful. Christ-Centered. Lose any one of these—and we drift.

1. Contextual: What Did It Mean Then, Before It Speaks Now?

The Bible was not written to 21st-century readers. It was written to real people, in real places, under real pressures.

To Israel in exile. To churches under persecution. To disciples surrounded by pagan temples. To believers who didn't have podcasts or commentaries—just scrolls and faith. Context doesn't distance the Bible from us—it roots it.

Contextual reading means asking:

- What did the writer mean in his culture, language, and moment?
- What was the Spirit addressing through this text—then?
- What was the setting, tension, covenant, and audience?

Only when we understand what it meant then Can we faithfully bring it into what it means now.

When we skip this, we distort:

- We turn promises into slogans
- We sever commands from their context
- We quote verses that contradict the paragraph

We do not need modern relevance. We need ancient faithfulness.

2. Careful: Let the Text Speak Before You Speak for It

God does not need hype. He requires holiness. A careful reader is not slow to believe. They are slow to assume.

This is not suspicion masked as scholarship. Careful reading is not endless deconstruction—it is disciplined devotion. It does not spiral into cynicism or treat the Bible as a code to be cracked. It listens with awe, examines with integrity, and submits with joy. Discernment is not doubt—it is reverence applied to reading.

They do not rush to tweetable insights or sermon-ready slogans. They wait. They weigh. They test.

"Be quick to hear, slow to speak..."—James 1:19

That applies to doctrine too.
Careful reading means:

- Don't build doctrine on one isolated verse
- Don't let unclear passages override the clear ones
- Don't weaponize one text to silence another
- Don't speak where God has not spoken

We are not editors. We are messengers. The text is not raw material for cleverness. It is revelation. Handle it as such.

3. Christ-Centered: The Point of Every Page

If your interpretation doesn't lead you to Christ—Start over. Jesus is not a cameo in the Old Testament. He is the thread, the substance, the destination.

> *"Beginning with Moses and all the Prophets, He explained to them the things concerning Himself in all the Scriptures."*—Luke 24:27

He is the fulfillment of the Law. The center of prophecy. The key to every covenant.

Christ-centered reading means:

- The Gospel is the spine of Scripture
- Promises find their "Yes" in Him
- Warnings point to Him
- Commands are shaped by His mercy and mission

This does not mean every verse mentions Jesus. It means every verse finds clarity in relation to Him.

Consider the Levitical laws—often dismissed as outdated rituals. Yet through Christ, the priesthood, sacrifice, and sanctuary all find fulfillment. The lamb without blemish points to the spotless Son. The Day of Atonement foreshadows the cross. Even the tabernacle reveals a God who dwells with His people. These were shadows—but Christ is the substance. And once He is seen, the Old Testament sings.

Do not interpret in ways that magnify man and minimize Christ. That is not faithfulness. That is flattery.

Do Not Go Beyond What Is Written

A HOUSE DIVIDED

> *"Do not go beyond what is written..."*
> —*1 Corinthians 4:6*

That's not restraint. That's reverence. Don't stretch the text to fit your system. Don't dilute it for acceptance. Don't twist it to match your tribe. And do not stay silent where the Word speaks plainly.

The Word Gives Light—to the Humble

> *"The unfolding of Your words gives light; it gives understanding to the simple."*—*Psalm 119:130*

It does not say:

> *"To the scholar."*
> *"To the intellectual."*
> *"To the seminary graduate."*

It says—to the simple. Those who tremble. Those who listen.

God has not hidden truth behind credentials. He has revealed it by His Spirit, through His Word, to the one who reads in submission.

The Watchman's Lens

You are not allowed to speculate recklessly. You are not permitted to manipulate Scripture to defend your stream. You are not sent to echo your tribe.

You are sent to guard the truth. To preach the Word. To see clearly, speak truthfully, and tremble rightly.

Your interpretive lens must be:
Contextual. Careful. Christ-Centered.

Anything less is not faithful stewardship. It is filtered religion.

Reflection: Integrity Over Insight

The Church does not need more clever exegesis. It needs more honest exegesis. Less performance. More precision. Less trend. More truth. Less self. More Scripture.

The Watchman's charge is not to be original. It is to be obedient. So interpret as one who will give account. Speak as one entrusted with flame. And above all—keep Christ at the center.

Lay Down the Pen. Pick Up the Word

We are drowning in commentary. Drowning in perspectives. Drowning in systems that explain the Word—before we've even read the Word. There is no shortage of devotionals. No lack of study Bibles. No absence of trusted teachers, movements, networks, and frameworks. And yet—in all the noise, the one voice that still speaks clearly is the one we filter the most.

> *"The word of God is living and active, sharper than any two-edged sword..."—Hebrews 4:12*

But we've dulled the edge. By tradition. By tribe. By trends. By fear of saying what God already said.

It's time to lay down the filter. And pick up the Word.

We've Grown Comfortable with Curated Theology

There is a kind of safety in inherited interpretation. In well-lit footnotes and familiar voices. In study tools and sermon outlines that tell us what the Bible must be saying.

And yet—curated theology often becomes predigested faith. It's easy to swallow. Hard to test. And even harder to unlearn when it's wrong.

We begin quoting our favorite preachers more than Christ. We defend our teachers more than truth. We rely on doctrinal summaries instead of wrestling through the raw weight of Scripture.

We call it discipleship. But sometimes it's just delegation. The early Church had no app. No podcast feed. No filters but fear of God and a scroll in hand. And they turned the world upside down.

The Filters We Bring—and Don't See

The most dangerous filter is the one you never notice.

- Doctrinal loyalty: "This is how we interpret that passage."
- Cultural pressure: "That can't mean what it says—it would offend."
- Experiential theology: "I haven't seen that, so it can't be real."
- Tribal identity: "My camp agrees. That settles it."
- Ministry protection: "If we preach that, we lose people."

Each of these begins with subtle fear— and ends in suppressed truth. What we forget is this: The Word is not fragile. It doesn't need spin. It needs space. Let it speak. Let it cut. Let it shine unfiltered.

Let the Word Cut Again

We do not need louder voices. We need sharper ones. The Word of God does not flatter our theology. It confronts it. It doesn't decorate our sermon slides. It divides between soul and spirit, between performance and purity.

We have read to support our brand. Now we must read to surrender our bias.

Don't ask,

> *"What does this passage say for my ministry?"*

Ask,

> *"What is God saying, whether or not it benefits my platform?"*

The Word Still Reforms

Every true awakening begins when filters fall.

Luther did not plan a movement. He read the Word without tradition's shadow.

Tyndale gave his life not for commentary, but for clarity.

Wesley preached holiness, not novelty. The Spirit moved—because the Word was unshackled. And it still reforms today. Not through social media. Not through systems. Not through spin. But through the ancient voice, spoken freshly to trembling hearts.

The Bible Was Never Meant to Be Shouted Over

We quote influencers. We defend footnotes. We shout labels: "heretic," "liberal," "legalist," "lukewarm." And all the while, the Bible remains—open. Waiting. Speaking.

But no one's listening.

> *"Be still, and know that I am God..."*
> —Psalm 46:10

Be still. Put down the doctrinal slogans. Close the commentary. Silence the algorithm. Pick up the Word again. And listen.

A HOUSE DIVIDED

The Word Will Unify What Man Has Fractured

We have fractured over:

- Eschatology
- Baptism
- Gifts
- Governance
- Creeds
- Commentaries
- Conferences

We have taken side notes and turned them into dividing walls. But when the Word is read plainly, in community, with humility and reverence— unity is possible again. Not because we erase conviction. But because we exalt Christ above our camps. When the Bible becomes a foundation again, the walls come down.

A Watchman's Charge

As a Watchman, you are not called to echo the noise. You are called to cut through it. You do not need to out-argue, out-publish, or out-perform. You need to return to the One voice that never falters. Lay down the filter— of fame, fear, denomination, identity.

Pick up the Word.
Let it speak first to you.
Let it cut you. Let it cleanse you. Let it burn away the assumptions you didn't know you were using. And when it has, speak.

Speak as one who has heard. Not from the tribe. Not from tradition. From the throne.

Reflection: One Voice Remains

When the filters fall... When the camps fade... When the commentaries grow quiet... One voice still thunders.

"Thus saith the Lord."

And that will be enough. Let it be enough for you. Let it be enough for the Church. Let it be enough for the next generation.
Pick up the Word. And don't flinch.

Watchman's Prayer

Lord, deliver us from filters that flatter our tribe. Guard us from systems that silence Your voice. Give us hunger like the Bereans —who searched, not scrolled. And let the simplicity of Christ shine through again. Let us not be famous for what we interpret —but faithful to what You have said.
In Jesus' name,
Amen.

5

When Truth Is Torn

A House Cannot Stand

A Torn Banner at the Gates

Every kingdom flies a banner. It is not just cloth. It is not just ornament. It is identity. A banner signals allegiance. It declares who rules the territory. It unites the people under a common authority, a common cause, a common truth. A whole banner proclaims: We are one. We are resolved. We are under command. A torn banner whispers something else: We are fractured. We are uncertain. We have forgotten who we are. And at the gates of the world's watching eyes, the Church's banner no longer flies as it should.

The Church Has a Banner

A HOUSE DIVIDED

We are not a people without a standard. The Church, from its inception, was marked not by swords or slogans—but by truth. Not just as an abstract doctrine. But as a Person.

> *"I am the way, the truth, and the life..."*
> *—John 14:6*

Truth is not a theological category. It is the King Himself. The Church marches not under a system, not under a denomination, not under a brand—but under Jesus, the Truth incarnate. He is the banner. The Scriptures are His standard. The Spirit is His seal. And unity under that banner is not a suggestion—it is our witness to the world.

> *"Sanctify them through thy truth: thy word is truth... that they all may be one... so that the world may believe that You have sent Me."*
> *—John 17:17, 21*

But the Banner Is Torn

What began as a pure declaration—Jesus is Lord—has been ripped by divisions. We still fly the banner. But it's frayed.

- Torn by theological rivalries.
- Ripped by doctrinal tribalism.
- Weathered by generational neglect.
- Pierced by compromise and cultural accommodation.

Instead of one clear cry—"Christ crucified, risen, and reigning"—we shout over each other with competing claims, campaigns, and confessions. The world no longer hears a single song. They hear a cacophony of contradictions. We say we are one Body. But our torn banner tells another story.

Truth Was Meant to Unify

Truth is not the enemy of unity. Truth is the foundation of it.

> *"You shall know the truth, and the truth shall make you free."—John 8:32*

Freedom does not come from theological flexibility. It comes from divine clarity. Jesus prayed, "Sanctify them in truth." Paul wrote, "Speak the truth in love." Peter exhorted, "Be established in the truth." But when the Church treats truth as optional, or merely interpretive, or worse—tribal—the result is not humility. It is confusion. And confusion kills witness.

When the Banner Is Torn, So Is Our Voice

There was a time when the Church spoke with weight. Not because it was politically aligned. Not because it was the majority. But because its banner was clear. The world might disagree, but they knew what the Church stood for:

- Christ crucified for sinners
- Scripture as final authority
- Holiness in lifestyle
- Boldness in proclamation
- Compassion rooted in truth

A HOUSE DIVIDED

But today? Ask ten churches the same question and get twelve answers. Not on secondary matters—but on primary ones.

- Is Scripture sufficient?
- What is the Gospel?
- What is marriage?
- What is sin?
- Who is Jesus?

These are not mysteries. They are not side issues. They are foundations. But our banner has been so torn by preference, performance, and pride that the world no longer knows what Christianity actually is.

We Still March—but Do We Still Witness?

The Church still gathers. Still sings. Still preaches. Still expands. But beneath which banner?

- The banner of cultural relevance?
- The banner of theological celebrity?
- The banner of denominational history?
- The banner of political alignment?

We still march. But does heaven recognize the flag we carry? And does the world? Not because we blend in—but because we stand out with a truth that does not tremble. A banner that does not change with trends, a message that is not mutilated by fear of offense.

A Banner Once Lifted on a Hill

There was once another banner. Lifted not at a gate,

but on a hill. Not made of cloth, but of wood and blood.

> *"And I, if I be lifted up, will draw all men unto Me."—John 12:32*

That was the banner. Christ crucified. Truth incarnate. Love without compromise. Justice without apology. Mercy without dilution. And that is still our banner—if we will return to it. If we will stop flying the flags of our factions and return to the cross, the Church might once again speak with a singular voice.

Reflection: The Banner Must Be Mended

A torn banner can be mended. But it cannot be mended by public relations or doctrinal diplomacy. It must be mended by repentance. By leaders returning to what is written, not what is marketable. By believers rejecting tribal loyalty in favor of biblical fidelity. By churches laying down the brand and lifting up the blood-stained cross. We do not need to redesign the banner. We need to raise it again. Not in pieces. Not in parts. Whole. Holy. Undeniable. The Church is not called to march beneath fractured convictions. We are called to march beneath a single, glorious, uncompromised declaration:

> *"Jesus is Lord."*

And His Word is truth. Let the banner fly again.

Unity Is Not Sentimental—It's Missional

The Strategy of Oneness in a Divided World. We have treated unity like a wedding centerpiece. A nice idea.

A HOUSE DIVIDED

An optional adornment. Beautiful when present, but nonessential when missing. We say things like:

> "Wouldn't it be nice if the Church could just be united?"

Or:

> "Someday, maybe, once all our doctrine is in place, we can come together."

But Jesus didn't speak of unity as an ornament. He treated it as oxygen. Not as a future luxury—but as a present strategy.

Unity Was Never an Add-On

The modern Church often treats unity as sentimental—a byproduct of agreement, a relational nicety, a bonus feature of mature faith. But in the Scriptures, unity is never described that way. Unity is not optional. It is not cosmetic. It is missional. It is how the world comes to believe the Gospel. Jesus made that abundantly clear:

> "Sanctify them in the truth; your word is truth... that they may all be one... so that the world may believe that you have sent me."
> —John 17:17, 21

Unity is not built on good feelings. It is built on truth. And when that truth is shared, when it sanctifies, when it unifies—it creates witness.

Truth Produces Unity. Unity Displays Truth.

Jesus prayed,

"Sanctify them in the truth. Your word is truth."

Not in sentiment. Not in tradition. Not in personality or culture. In the Word. In truth. That truth:

- Cleanses our hearts
- Aligns our minds
- Breaks our pride
- Binds us together

Then, having been sanctified, Jesus continues:

"That they may all be one... so that the world may believe."

Truth leads to unity. Unity leads to credibility. Credibility leads to faith. This is not sentimentalism. This is strategy. When the Church is fractured, the world questions the truth. When the Church is one, the world sees a living Gospel.

Disunity Is Not Just Unfortunate—It's Disobedient

We often think of division as regrettable but understandable.

"Doctrinal differences are just a fact of life,"

we say.

"We're never going to agree on everything."

But that misses the point. Yes, some disagreements are inevitable. But division is not inevitable—it is disobedient. Because when truth is decentralized into tribes and slogans and brands, the world does not see the Cross. They see competition.

A HOUSE DIVIDED

They see contradiction. And they walk away. Jesus did not say the world would believe because of our cleverness. He said the world would believe because of our unity in truth.

Division Erodes Credibility

Every split in the Church costs something. Every denominational rivalry. Every tribal argument over secondary issues. Every podcast war. Every theological slander thread on social media. It chips away at the foundation.

- Our credibility erodes.
- Our testimony grows confused.
- Our Gospel becomes suspect.

We are called to preach one message, about one Savior, through one Spirit, grounded in one Word—yet we deliver it as if it came from different publishers. When our house is divided, our Gospel becomes muddled. And a muddled Gospel is not compelling. It is dismissed.

A Divided Church Cannot Stand

Jesus said:

> *"Every kingdom divided against itself is laid waste. And a house divided against itself will not stand."—Matthew 12:25*

That applies to more than political movements. It applies to the Church. We are not immune. Our witness is not untouchable. Our mission is not self-sustaining. The early Church grew—not because it had perfected doctrine in every category, but because it had clarity on the essentials and unity in the Spirit. They were of "one accord." They were "devoted to the apostles' teaching." They were willing to suffer for the truth—together. That unity had weight. It bore witness to something supernatural. The world didn't just hear the message—they saw it embodied.

Truth Must Define Unity—Not Compromise

Let's be clear: unity at the cost of truth is not unity. It's sentimentalism. It's a fragile ceasefire built on shallow agreements. Biblical unity is not built by ignoring doctrine. It is built by agreeing on what God has made clear, and refusing to divide over what He has allowed freedom in. That means:

- Holding fast to the Gospel
- Agreeing on the authority of Scripture
- Upholding Christ as the center
- Refusing to fracture over timelines, gifts, or governance structures

Unity does not erase nuance. It puts nuance in its place—beneath the throne of Jesus.

A Divided Truth Cannot Save

Here is the warning: If the Church continues to divide over non-essentials, we are not just weakening our voice. We are distorting the message. Because a divided truth does not invite salvation—it invites skepticism. Imagine telling a skeptic:

> *"God loves you. But depending on the church, that may mean different things."*

A HOUSE DIVIDED

"Jesus saves—but what exactly that salvation is depends on which camp you're talking to."
"We believe the Bible is enough. Well, except where our tradition adds to it."

This is not good news. It's religious noise. And Jesus didn't die to produce noise. He died to declare a message of reconciliation.

Reflection: Unity as Strategy, Not Sentiment

Unity is not a postscript. It's not an optional virtue. It is the means by which the world sees Jesus. The world doesn't just want to know what we believe. They want to know if it's real. They are watching: Do we love one another? Do we bear with one another? Do we stand under the same banner, or fly our own? Unity in truth is how we say: Yes, He is real. Yes, the Gospel is one. Yes, we are sent—not by systems, but by the Savior. And we walk as one.

John 17 as the Intercession That Should Still Echo

The Forgotten Prayer That Still Holds the Church Together

Jesus didn't pray for church growth. He didn't pray for political power. He didn't ask the Father for religious branding, denominational strength, or cultural influence.

He prayed for oneness.

> *"That they may all be one, just as you, Father, are in me, and I in you... so that the world may believe that you have sent me."—John 17:21*

This was not a side prayer. It wasn't a poetic conclusion to a powerful ministry. It was the last recorded intercession of Jesus before His crucifixion and it was all about unity.

Not superficial harmony. Not sentimental togetherness. A unity rooted in the very nature of the Trinity.

The Unity Jesus Prayed For Was Theological, Not Just Relational

Jesus could have prayed for many things. He could have prayed for courage in persecution. For organizational strength. For doctrinal sophistication. For moral resilience.

But He prayed that His followers would be one. Not just one in friendship, but one in truth.

> *"Sanctify them in the truth; your word is truth."—John 17:17*

The unity Jesus described isn't a lowest-common-denominator peace treaty. It's not about ignoring differences. It's about being sanctified—set apart, made holy—by truth. And that truth is not abstract. It's not floating in ambiguity. It's written, revealed, preserved.

> *"Your word is truth."*

Submit for Sanctification And Be One

Unity is the result of sanctification, and sanctification comes through submission to the Word of God. This is not a call for unity through compromise. This is a call for unity through clarity.

A HOUSE DIVIDED

Jesus prayed that His people would be united as He is united with the Father. How is the Trinity one?

- In essence.
- In purpose.
- In truth.
- In love.

That's not shallow unity. That's holy union. And that's what the Church is meant to reflect. But we can't reflect the oneness of the Trinity if we're each submitting to a different source of truth.

If one church submits to Scripture, another to tradition, another to cultural mood, and another to personal experience, we will never be one in the way Jesus prayed for.

Unity requires one authority. And that authority must be the Word of God.

The Enemy Doesn't Just Tempt—He Divides

There is a reason why Satan's first recorded action in human history was to question the Word of God:

"Did God really say...?"—Genesis 3:1

The serpent's strategy has not changed. He knows that the fastest way to destroy a mission is to divide the messengers.

If he can:

- Turn believers against one another...
- Inject doctrinal confusion...
- Make tribalism feel like conviction...
- Twist the Word just enough to sow doubt...

...then the Church will be too distracted to stand,

too fragmented to speak, and too divided to shine. He doesn't need to burn our Bibles. He just needs to keep us arguing about what they mean.

Because a Unified Church Is Dangerous

Satan is not afraid of talent. He is not afraid of programs. He is not afraid of content creation or denominational expansion.

He is afraid of a Church that is one in Christ, one in truth, and one in purpose.

- A unified Church speaks with power.
- A unified Church is hard to manipulate.
- A unified Church is unshakable in persecution.
- A unified Church cannot be bought, silenced, or seduced.

When believers are aligned under the Word, filled with the Spirit, and committed to the Gospel—hell trembles. That's why Jesus prayed what He did. Because He knew what was at stake.

And a Fractured Church Is Easy to Distract

But what happens when we forget that prayer? What happens when we redefine unity as "agreeing to disagree"? Or when we exalt system over Scripture, denomination over discipleship, or preference over principle?

The Church becomes fractured. And fracture always leads to compromise. Because the more we divide, the more we feel the need to soften the message. We dilute truth to keep the peace. We silence conviction to protect unity. And eventually, we lose both. A fractured Church is not just confused. It's weak.

- Its message lacks clarity.
- Its people lack confidence.
- Its witness lacks credibility.

John 17 Wasn't Just a Prayer—It Was a Strategy

Jesus wasn't praying in generalities. He was praying missionally.

> *"...that the world may believe that You have sent Me."—John 17:21*

The unity of the Church is not just for the Church. It is for the world. Our unity under truth is the evidence that Jesus is who He said He is. It is the apologetic the world is starving for. And we are silencing that apologetic every time we choose division over submission, pride over sanctification, or systems over Scripture.

Reflection: Let His Prayer Become Ours

The intercession of John 17 still echoes. It echoed in the upper room. It echoed in Gethsemane. It echoed at the cross, where blood sanctified the ones He prayed for.

And it must echo in us.

Let it shape our preaching. Let it guide our discernment. Let it convict our pride. Because Jesus didn't ask the Father to make us impressive. He asked Him to make us one.

And that prayer is still our assignment.

When Doctrinal Fracture Becomes Spiritual Failure

The fracture didn't start with scandal. It didn't begin with corruption or compromise. It began—quietly—with confusion over truth. It began when we took what God had made plain and turned it into tribal distinctions. When we elevated preferences into platforms. When we baptized marketing strategies in theological language and called it conviction. And now, the fracture runs deep.

Confusion Within the Household of Faith

Consider these images. They are not extreme. They are commonplace. A preacher declares that God's grace is irresistible—that the elect will be drawn and saved by sovereign decree. Another insists that grace must be freely received—that to reject it is a tragic, human choice. One church calls baptism essential for salvation—a moment of regeneration. Another calls it symbolic—a testimony, not a sacrament. Some preach the gifts of the Spirit with passion—tongues, prophecy, healing, miracles. Others warn against emotional manipulation and theological drift. And yet all of them claim:

- The same Bible
- The same Gospel
- The same Christ

To the outside world, the contradictions are not subtle. They are loud. And they are costly.

A HOUSE DIVIDED

The Result? Spiritual Fallout

We are witnessing the consequences in real time:

1. Deconstruction.

Many young believers aren't walking away from God—they're walking away from confusion. Raised in churches that can't agree on truth, they see contradiction where they expected clarity. So they deconstruct—not in rebellion, but in despair.

2. Division.

Churches split not over heresy—but over style, tone, and secondary doctrine.

- Worship becomes warfare.
- Eschatology becomes isolation.
- Spiritual gifts become political lines.
- Baptism becomes battleground instead of blessing.

We divide over what should remain in-house disagreements. And we divide so often that we've stopped mourning the split.

3. Distrust.

The watching world no longer sees conviction. They see contradiction. They hear one church preach the exclusivity of Christ, and another preach tolerance of all paths. They hear one pastor proclaim that sin must be repented of, and another say it must be redefined. And the result is mistrust. Not just of us. But of the message we carry.

4. Dilution.

To avoid division, many churches adapt the message. They preach to keep the peace, not to pierce the heart. And in the name of unity, we sacrifice clarity.

- Sin is renamed "brokenness."
- Hell is erased.
- Conviction is replaced by self-help.
- The cross becomes an option, not a necessity.

In our attempt to avoid theological confrontation, we have embraced spiritual compromise.

When Personality Replaces Principle

Even among sincere believers, tribalism thrives. Not because we intend it—but because we have turned pastors into platforms and teachers into tribes. We hear it in subtle phrases:

> *"I follow Piper..."*
> *"I follow MacArthur..."*
> *"I follow Chandler..."*
> *"I follow Beth Moore..."*
> *"I follow Tim Keller..."*

It echoes Corinth:

> *"I follow Paul... I follow Apollos..."*
> —1 Corinthians 1:12

And Paul's response remains:

> *"Is Christ divided?"*—1 Corinthians 1:13

We have done what the early Church was warned

not to do. We have made doctrine a branding tool. We have made theological distinction a marketing strategy. And in doing so, we've taken what was meant to build the Church and turned it into a way to segregate the saints.

We've Made Truth a Preference

We say things like:

> *"That's not my theological stream."*
> *"That's not how we interpret it at our church."*
> *"That's not the tradition I was raised in."*

And while those statements are understandable, they expose a deeper issue. We've made truth subjective. We've turned it into a preference. A flavor. A denomination. But truth is not tribal. Truth is unchanging, rooted in the Word of God, not the camp of man.

This Is Not Merely Doctrinal—It's Spiritual

What begins as theological fracture becomes spiritual failure.

- When clarity is lost, holiness decays.
- When doctrine is muddled, obedience becomes optional.
- When truth becomes tribal, unity becomes impossible.

And worst of all: The power of the Gospel is muted.

We preach Christ crucified. But when that

message is surrounded by a dozen competing voices, each carrying their own doctrinal baggage, the cross gets lost in the noise.

What We Sow into the Soil of the Church

When we make doctrine a dividing line over what God calls disputable, we sow confusion. When we elevate tradition over text, we sow distrust. When we prioritize branding over biblical clarity, we sow dilution. And what grows from that soil is not fruit—but factions.

The Church becomes a network of competing ministries, personalities, and platforms. Each with their own language, loyalties, and liturgies.

But the cross? It calls us to die to all of that.

Reflection: From Fracture to Faithfulness

Paul pleaded with the Church in Corinth—not to abandon conviction, but to anchor it in Christ alone.

> *"Has Christ been divided? Was Paul crucified for you? Or were you baptized in the name of Paul?"—1 Corinthians 1:13*

That question echoes still. Was Piper crucified for you? Was Keller raised for you? Was your system nailed to a tree?

No.

Christ was. And that must be enough. Let us end the confusion. Let us silence the tribal loyalty. Let us raise not a denomination, not a brand, but the truth of the Gospel—whole, holy, and undivided. Because when the Church speaks with one voice again, the world may finally hear it.

A HOUSE DIVIDED

The Devil Doesn't Have to Destroy the Church

Why Confusion Is the Enemy's Most Effective Weapon?

Satan rarely attacks with fire. He attacks with fog. He doesn't always roar. He whispers. Not always with persecution, but with pride. Not always with lies, but with distortions. He blurs the lines. Not to erase the Church, but to weaken it from within. And we, all too often, unknowingly help him do it.

The Strategy of the Serpent: Divide, Then Conquer

From the Garden to today, the enemy's plan has remained consistent.

- In Eden, he didn't begin with rebellion. He began with a question: "Did God really say…?"
- In the wilderness, he quoted Scripture—not to affirm, but to twist.
- In the early Church, he didn't silence the apostles with swords. He infiltrated with false brethren, false teachers, and factionalism.

Satan knows what many churches have forgotten: A house divided cannot stand. (Matthew 12:25) He doesn't need to destroy the Church outright. He only needs to keep us divided long enough to make us ineffective.

He Blurs Truth Just Enough to Cause Suspicion

The devil doesn't often launch a frontal assault on doctrine. Instead, he causes doubt to creep in.

"Is this passage really essential?"

"Is that view outdated?"
"Did God really mean that?"
"What if there's another way to interpret this that's less offensive?"

And so he begins to fog the clarity of Scripture, not by open contradiction, but by introducing enough ambiguity to splinter confidence. Where there was once conviction, now there's confusion. Where there was once clarity, now there's camps. Where there was once shared truth, now there's tribal interpretation.

He Stokes Pride Just Enough to Fuel Division

Satan doesn't always tempt with immorality. Sometimes he tempts with identity.

He whispers:

"You're more faithful than them."
"Your interpretation is more pure."
"Your stream is more Spirit-filled."
"Your denomination honors the Bible better."

And instead of rejoicing in the Gospel, we begin to boast in our tribe. Instead of defending truth, we begin defending our system. Instead of bearing with one another, we begin building walls. This is not theological boldness. It's spiritual blindness. And the devil uses it to great effect.

He Plants False Teachers

False teaching doesn't always show up wrapped in heresy. Sometimes, it shows up wrapped in charisma.

A HOUSE DIVIDED

- Teachers who can quote Scripture but never submit to it.
- Leaders who preach the Gospel but center themselves.
- Pastors who are more platform-driven than Word-driven.

These are not always wolves. Sometimes, they're shepherds who have lost their way—drifting from truth into self-importance.

Paul warned Timothy not only of false doctrine—but of teachers

> *"desiring to be teachers of the law, without understanding"—1 Timothy 1:7*

That warning still stands. Ego may not break orthodoxy immediately. But it fractures unity by turning pulpits into pedestals—and followers into factions.

And We Participate

The enemy doesn't divide the Church alone. He enlists our help—subtly, incrementally, and tragically. We participate when:

- We refuse correction, convinced that our perspective is untouchable.
- We idolize our tradition, treating denominational heritage as sacred text.
- We weaponize our preferences, forcing matters of style and conscience into matters of fellowship.
- We label fellow believers as enemies, instead of family to reason with and restore.

This is not spiritual discernment. This is spiritual sabotage. And the devil smiles at our zeal—so long as it keeps us at war with one another.

Division Is Not Just Doctrinal Drift. It's Spiritual Sabotage.

We often think division is merely a theological problem. But division is a spiritual attack—a direct assault on the body of Christ.

> *"God is not a God of confusion, but of peace."*
> *—1 Corinthians 14:33*

Where confusion reigns, God is not honored. Every church split, every public controversy, every unresolved debate—when left unchecked—amplifies the voice of the enemy. Not because we disagreed. But because we let division become identity, instead of pressing into truth together.

This Is Not a Call for Unity at All Costs

Let's be clear:

- This is not a call to abandon doctrine.
- This is not a plea to embrace compromise.
- This is not a demand for theological silence.

Truth matters. Conviction is essential. Rebuking error is biblical. But we must also recognize this: Disunity always costs more than we think. It costs our credibility. It costs our peace. It costs our witness. And it costs us our spiritual authority.

What Division Actually Costs

A HOUSE DIVIDED

When we divide over secondary matters and elevate preferences to the level of doctrine, we:

- Undermine the beauty of unity that Jesus prayed for (John 17)
- Weaken our apologetic—because a fractured Church makes a fragile Gospel
- Confuse the next generation, who will inherit our disputes but not our clarity
- Empower the enemy, who thrives in uncorrected confusion

This is not overstatement. This is reality. Churches are closing. Believers are deconstructing. The world is watching. And Satan is not burning our pulpits—he's corrupting them with division.

Reflection: Recognize the Scheme. Resist the Split.

Paul wrote:

> *"We are not ignorant of his schemes."*
> *—2 Corinthians 2:11*

But many of us are. We don't see doctrinal division as warfare. We see it as

> *"just part of church life."*

We shrug at fragmentation as if it's unavoidable. But a Watchman doesn't shrug. A Watchman sounds the alarm—not to erase disagreement, but to restore truth and protect the flock. We must learn to recognize when the enemy is stirring the fog—when suspicion, ego, and rivalry threaten to replace clarity, humility, and fellowship. Division is not just sad. It's strategic.

And the only way to resist it is to return—again and again—to the Word that sanctifies, the truth that unifies, and the Christ who reigns over all tribes, tongues, and traditions.

Wounding Both Truth and Unity by Separation

The Church is often torn between two fears. On one side: Compromise. We fear losing truth in a sea of soft theology, watered-down preaching, and sentimental unity that avoids hard questions. On the other side: Division. We fear conflict, theological tribalism, and a fractured witness. We fear becoming the kind of Christians who use doctrine as a weapon and fellowship as a privilege granted only to those who agree with us.

So we drift. Some abandon truth to protect relationships. Others abandon relationships to protect truth. But both reactions wound the Body. Because truth and unity are not enemies. They are partners in sanctification.

Two Ditches—Both Dangerous

Some have tried to preserve unity by compromising truth. They minimize doctrine. They avoid controversy. They confuse silence with love. But unity without truth is not unity—it's sentimentality. It cannot sustain conviction. It cannot correct error. It cannot carry the cross. Others have tried to preserve truth by forsaking unity. They draw rigid lines. They break fellowship quickly. They elevate every disagreement to division. But truth without unity becomes arrogance. It loses compassion. It forgets grace. It mimics Pharisees more than Christ. Paul warned against both.

> *"Speaking the truth in love, we are to grow up in every way into him who is the head, into Christ..."—Ephesians 4:15*

This is not a balance to be struck. It's a maturity to be cultivated. We are not called to choose between truth and love, between clarity and community. We are called to grow up—into Christ—by holding them together.

Unity Without Truth Is Fragile

There is a form of unity that feels warm but crumbles under pressure. It values agreement more than alignment. It hides disagreement for the sake of peace. It often says, "Let's not get too theological." But here's the problem: real unity requires real foundations.

If your unity cannot survive doctrinal confrontation, it is not biblical unity. It is a social contract. It avoids division not through sanctification, but through avoidance. And over time, that avoidance grows into doctrinal apathy. We cannot unify around uncertainty. The Church must be "the pillar and buttress of the truth" (1 Timothy 3:15). Without truth, our oneness is only cosmetic.

Truth Without Unity Is Cold

But there's another danger—just as real. Some pursue truth with such intensity that they forget why truth matters in the first place. They argue not to edify, but to win. They correct not to restore, but to prove superiority. They speak truth—but without love, patience, or discernment.

And what happens?

Truth becomes an idol, used to justify harshness. Doctrinal precision becomes a substitute for spiritual maturity. People become categories. Discipleship becomes debate.

This too is immaturity.

> *"If I have prophetic powers, and understand all mysteries and all knowledge... but have not love, I am nothing."—1 Corinthians 13:2*

Truth must not lose its shape. But it must never lose its heart.

Truth and Unity Must Walk Together

These are not parallel paths. They are intertwined. Jesus prayed, "Sanctify them in the truth... that they may all be one." (John 17) Paul wrote, "One Lord, one faith, one baptism..." (Ephesians 4) Truth and unity are not two pursuits. They are two results of the same reality: being conformed to Christ.

To pursue truth is to love the Body. To love the Body is to guard the truth. Because truth protects the Church from error. And unity protects the Church from isolation. Together, they make the Gospel visible.

What This Looks Like Practically

So how do we live this? Here's what mature discernment requires:

- Speak with boldness and gentleness.

Truth should never be vague—but neither should it be harsh.
Say what Scripture says, without apology—but also without arrogance.

- Contend without quarrels.

"The Lord's servant must not be quarrelsome but kind to everyone..." —2 Timothy 2:24

We must defend truth without delighting in combat.

- Test every spirit, but not condemn every brother.

    Discernment is not suspicion.
    We are called to be wise, not paranoid.
    Correction is biblical. Accusation is not.

- Draw lines for protection, not preference.

We must separate from heresy—but not from every difference. Not all disagreements are departures from the faith.

Love Is the Context for Truth

Truth spoken without love is noise. Love expressed without truth is fraud. We speak truth because we love people. We love people by telling them the truth. But we also walk with them, even when they're not yet where we are. We make room for growth, not uniformity.

Love does not demand silence. Love invites truth. And then walks patiently beside it.

Reflection: Mature Together or Divide Apart

Truth and unity are not in competition. They are companions on the road to maturity. You cannot guard truth by isolating yourself from the Body. And you cannot protect unity by hiding from correction. Both require courage. Both require humility. Both require the Spirit. And both are required if we are to grow into the full stature of Christ.

Let us be a people:

- Clear in doctrine
- Gentle in tone
- Unyielding in conviction
- Unashamed in compassion

Because when truth and unity walk hand in hand, the Church does more than survive. It becomes a witness the world cannot ignore.

Mend the Banner. Repair the Breach

The banner of truth still flies. Not as proudly. Not as visibly. Not as unanimously as it once did. But it flies. It is torn—yes. Frayed by division. Weathered by conflict. Stained by compromise. But it is not beyond repair. Because truth does not age. Truth does not fracture. Truth remains—eternal, unshaken, and always able to restore what we have broken.

The Breach Is Real—But It Is Not Irreparable

A HOUSE DIVIDED

It would be easy to despair. To look at the splintered condition of the Church and conclude the fracture is final.

There are over 45,000 denominations worldwide. Entire theological tribes speak past one another, not with malice, but with unexamined assumptions. Churches avoid doctrinal depth to avoid division. Others deepen division by equating minor disagreements with apostasy. But the breach, as real as it is, can be repaired.

God is not calling His people to retreat into silence, nor to escalate in sectarianism. We've seen glimpses of what rebuilding can look like. The Lausanne Movement brought together leaders from across the global Church—rooted in Gospel clarity and united in mission. The early creeds like Nicene and Chalcedonian didn't erase every difference—but they guarded the essentials. Even today, Gospel-centered coalitions show that theological diversity need not destroy doctrinal fidelity. These aren't perfect models—but they are proof that unity anchored in truth is possible.

He is calling us to rebuild.

> *"They shall raise up the former devastations; they shall repair the ruined cities, the devastations of many generations."*
> *—Isaiah 61:4*

The work of repair is not beneath us. It is the prophetic task of the faithful.

Now Is the Time to Rebuild

This is not the hour for retreat. This is not the

moment to celebrate our theological echo chambers. This is the moment to pick up the thread, take hold of the torn fabric, and begin to mend what division has destroyed. That rebuilding begins in three places:

1. Rebuilding Trust Across Traditions

There is a way to hold truth without isolating those who name the same Christ.

We must stop assuming that every difference is rebellion. Stop painting all disagreement as danger. Stop retreating into tribal pride.

Pursue understanding—not to adopt every view, but to learn. Unity doesn't require uniformity, but it does demand humility. What if we stopped weaponizing phrases like "biblical" as a code for "my view only"? What if we honored those who differ, as long as they remain tethered to the cross, the resurrection, and the Word of God?

Cooperation must never come at the cost of clarity. Fellowship is possible across traditions—but only where Christ is truly confessed: crucified, risen, and reigning; the only way to the Father; revealed in the Scriptures and exalted as Lord. Without that confession, unity becomes confusion.

Trust does not mean theological compromise. It means believing the best of others until proven otherwise. It means loving the Body—not just the part you're familiar with.

2. Rebuilding Clarity in Core Doctrine

We have majored on minors, while neglecting the foundations.

- Salvation by grace through faith

- The authority and sufficiency of Scripture
- The triune nature of God
- The bodily resurrection of Christ
- The exclusivity of Christ as Savior
- The indwelling power of the Holy Spirit
- The visible return of the King
- These are not blurry lines.

They are non-negotiables. They are the beams of the banner we must lift again—together. Instead of muddying the Gospel with denominational emphasis, let us preach it with apostolic clarity. And let our pulpits be known not for which movement we support, but for which message we will never stop proclaiming.

3. Rebuilding Bridges Where Walls Were Never Commanded

Some walls in the Church were built by God—walls of holiness, purity, and sound doctrine. But many others were built by us. Walls of tradition. Walls of style. Walls of suspicion. Walls that protect preferences, not purity. Where Scripture has not commanded division, we must stop creating it.

- Stop assuming reformed and charismatic cannot coexist under the Lordship of Christ.
- Stop thinking liturgy and spontaneity are signs of faithfulness or failure.
- Stop defining "sound" preaching by volume or vocabulary.

If Christ is not divided, why are we?

Conviction Is Not the Enemy—Pride Is

This is not a call to abandon conviction. Conviction is essential. It is the backbone of courage. But conviction without humility becomes heresy in disguise.

We must wield conviction as a sword of truth, not a club of self-righteousness. We must be a people who:

- Contend, but not quarrel.
- Test, but not tear down.
- Correct, but not cancel.
- Hold fast, but also hold out our hand to those willing to walk in the same direction.

The strongest builders are not those who shout the loudest, but those who bend down to do the quiet work of repair.

The Watchman's Role in the Breach

The watchman is not passive. He does not scroll through theological controversy with detachment. He does not excuse fracture as "just the way things are." He doesn't confuse outrage for obedience. He watches. He warns. And then—he works. He repairs what others overlooked. He weeps over what others mocked. He calls the people back—not to nostalgia, but to truth and unity as Christ defined them. He stands on the wall, not to judge those inside, but to guard the truth within and call the Church to unity without compromise.

Reflection: Lets Acknowledge to Rebuild

If we pretend the banner isn't torn, we will never mend it. If we minimize the breach, we will never repair it. If we excuse division as inevitable, we will never

A HOUSE DIVIDED

reverse it. But if we see it for what it is—a spiritual emergency—then the rebuilding can begin. So let us:

- Mend the banner of truth—by lifting it higher than our factions
- Repair the breach in fellowship—by returning to shared essentials
- And walk humbly as Watchmen, guarding the wall with truth in one hand and love in the other

Because Jesus is coming for a unified Bride. And now is the time to prepare her garments.

Watchman's Prayer:

Lord, let us feel what You felt when You prayed for unity. Let us see the breach not as strategy, but as sin. Let us speak truth, not just to power, but to each other. Mend what we have torn. And let the world see You—undistorted by our division.
    In Jesus' name,
    Amen.

6

DISCERNING TRUTH IN A NOISY CHURCH

Spiritual Maturity & The Call to Test Every Teaching

A Choir of Discordant Voices

The modern Church swims in a flood of content. Streams. Sermons. Podcasts. Panels. Prophets. TikTok theologians. Instagram apologetics. YouTube exposés. Short-form "truth bombs" dressed as wisdom. Long-form theology laced with agendas. Reels. Reels. Reels.

Each voice demands attention. Each message claims authority. Each delivery is optimized for engagement, virality, and influence. And amidst the noise, we find ourselves not just overwhelmed—but disoriented.

It's no longer enough to ask, "What is being said?" We must now ask, "Is this faithful? Is this true? Is this centered on Christ?" Because in this age, truth is not always louder. Often it is quieter. Sometimes it is humbler. Almost always—it is more costly to follow.

This is where discernment becomes essential.

Discernment is Spirit-formed perception—shaped by Scripture, centered on Christ, and exercised through humble obedience. It is not suspicion dressed as wisdom. It is not cold analysis. It is the spiritual maturity to recognize the difference between what sounds good and what is truly godly. However, lets not confused this discernment with true Discernment which is guided by the Holy Spirit.

The Marketplace of Theology

The digital age has democratized the pulpit. Anyone with a Bible verse and a microphone can gather a following. Anyone with charisma and editing software can create the illusion of authority.

This is not inherently wrong. Many faithful teachers today speak through screens. But in a world where every voice shouts with equal volume, the Church often forgets to ask: Who is speaking with fidelity?

We're no longer choosing between truth and error. We're discerning between true and almost-true. Between biblical and Bible-sounding. Between Christ-exalting and self-enhancing. And in the clamor of contradiction, clarity gets buried.

Truth Doesn't Compete with Volume

There is a spiritual law beneath the surface of our age: Volume is not the same as veracity.

Just because a message goes viral doesn't mean it comes from the Vine. Just because it resonates doesn't mean it roots. Just because it feels right doesn't mean it is right.

The Church must remember: The Word of the Lord does not always come with a shout. Often, it arrives as a whisper.

Elijah learned this in 1 Kings 19. Not in the wind. Not in the earthquake. Not in the fire. But in a still, small voice. And that same stillness still speaks today. But only the quieted soul can hear it.

The Danger of Emotional Clarity

We are drawn to what moves us. That is not inherently wrong—emotion is a gift. But in this generation, emotion has become the metric for truth.

> *"That sermon really spoke to me."*
> *"I felt the presence of God during that livestream."*
> *"This message gave me goosebumps."*
> *"She said what we've all been thinking."*

But none of those reactions validate the message. Truth is not measured by your spine. It is measured by Scripture.

In a Church flooded with emotional content, the challenge is no longer spotting what's false. It's locating what's faithful. Not just what is well-received— But what is well-rooted.

When Every Voice Sounds Right

This is the true tension of our age: When every voice sounds right, discernment is no longer optional—it's survival.

False teaching today rarely arrives dressed in heresy. It comes cloaked in nuance. It quotes Scripture. It uses "Jesus" as a tagline. It mirrors biblical language—but alters the core.

- It preaches "freedom" without repentance.
- It affirms "purpose" without confronting sin.
- It inspires self-love, but never calls for self-denial.
- It promises resurrection, but skips crucifixion.

These are not obvious errors. They are subtle rewrites of the true melody. And if you don't know the original tune—you'll follow the wrong choir.

The New Noise: Spiritual Content as a Substitute for Spiritual Depth

One of the greatest dangers facing the Church today is this: We are mistaking access for maturity. Because we have sermons, podcasts, reels, and devotionals at our fingertips, we assume we are spiritually grounded. But consumption is not cultivation.

- Listening to preaching is not the same as studying Scripture.
- Feeling conviction in a reel is not the same as submitting to correction.
- Agreeing with sound teaching is not the same as living by it—especially when it costs us.

We are not underfed. We are overstimulated and under-rooted. We've confused spiritual content with spiritual formation.

The Church Is a Choir—But We've Lost Our Sheet Music

The Church was never meant to be a collection of soloists. We are a choir. Not just a gathering of voices—but a harmony of truth. Our unity was meant to echo the same melody: the Word of God.

But in this generation?

- The sheet music is neglected.
- Scripture is clipped for soundbites.
- Doctrine is filtered through platforms.
- The melody is remixed for engagement.

The Word has become background noise to the voices we prefer. And the result?

- Doctrinal dissonance
- Theological confusion
- Moral fatigue
- Spiritual apathy

We've replaced the plumb line with applause—and then wondered why the walls tilt.

Arrival in a Generation of Static

This is the generation of static. Not silence. Not persecution. Not absence. Static. Constant motion. Constant content. Constant stimulation. And into the static, Christ still calls:

"My sheep hear My voice."—John 10:27

But His voice does not compete. It does not conform to algorithmic cadence. It does not shout to drown out the reels, the rage, the reels again. His voice is steady. Still. Scripture-rooted. Spirit-empowered. And those who follow Him must re-learn how to listen.

This chapter does not teach you how to be louder. It teaches you how to be still. To hear again. To test what is said. To rediscover what is written. Because discernment does not begin with outrage. It begins with attentiveness.

A HOUSE DIVIDED

Reflection: The Arrival of the Watchman's Responsibility

To discern in this age is not to become harsh. It is to become holy. To listen well. To test humbly. To warn without arrogance. To protect without pride. Because when every choir is singing their own song, the world needs to hear one voice again: The voice of the Shepherd through His Word. And the Watchman must not lose the melody.

Discernment Is Spiritual Maturity in Action

In a Church age marked by content overload, theological drift, and spiritual confusion, discernment is no longer a bonus skill—it is a core expression of obedience.

Discernment is not the domain of the elite. It is not spiritual snobbery. It is not a ministry for the suspicious. It is the fruit of maturity, and more importantly—it is a biblical command.

> *"But solid food is for the mature, for those who have their powers of discernment trained by constant practice to distinguish good from evil."*
> *—Hebrews 5:14*

This is the heartbeat of mature Christianity: constant training. Active discernment. The ability to distinguish not just between good and evil, but between almost true and truly faithful.

Discernment Is Not Judgmentalism—It's Obedience

In today's spiritually tolerant culture, the word "discernment" often carries baggage. It is misunderstood as divisive, judgmental, or ungracious. But Scripture does not treat it that way.

Discernment is not about condemning people. It's about testing messages. It's not a ministry of suspicion. It's a ministry of clarity.

Paul commands the Thessalonians:

> *"Test everything; hold fast what is good. Abstain from every form of evil."*
> —*1 Thessalonians 5:21–22*

To test everything is not an act of cynicism—it is an act of faithfulness. It demonstrates that we value God's Word above popular voices, viral theology, or emotional appeal.

Discernment Is Not a Gift for the Few—It's a Discipline for All

Some think of discernment as a spiritual gift given to a few especially perceptive believers. But in Hebrews, Paul ties discernment to spiritual diet. To maturity. To believers who have graduated from milk to meat.

Discernment is trained, not downloaded. It is developed, not assumed. And it's developed through constant use.

- Constant Scripture intake
- Constant comparison of teaching to truth
- Constant listening through the lens of the Gospel
- Constant prayer and dependence on the Spirit

This means discernment is within reach—for every Christian who desires maturity.

The Bereans: A Model of Biblical Discernment

One of the most underrated portraits of discernment in Scripture comes from Acts 17:

> *"Now these Jews were more noble than those in Thessalonica; they received the word with all eagerness, examining the Scriptures daily to see if these things were so."—Acts 17:11*

They were noble. Not because they blindly accepted the message. And not because they rejected it. They were noble because they tested it. They searched the Scriptures daily—not just to defend their traditions, but to see if what Paul was preaching aligned with God's Word. They didn't assume the worst. They didn't embrace without caution. They tested with humility. And the Spirit honored it.

Contrast that with our current culture, where some believers accept any message that resonates emotionally, and others reject anything that doesn't fit their tribal system. The Bereans show us a better way: Discernment driven by eagerness, filtered through the Word, and anchored in truth.

Discernment Protects More Than Doctrine

Discernment is not just about protecting theological statements. It's about protecting the Gospel itself.

Paul's warning in Galatians is striking:

> *"I am astonished that you are so quickly deserting him who called you in the grace of Christ and are turning to a different gospel..."—Galatians 1:6*

False teaching doesn't just alter ideas. It distorts the message of salvation. If we fail to discern, we fail to guard the Gospel.

Discernment defends:

- The truth of the cross

- The necessity of repentance
- The glory of Christ over man
- The sufficiency of Scripture
- The essence of grace

Without it, we drift—not always into heresy, but into powerless belief. And powerless belief produces spiritual apathy and confusion.

Discernment Is Sanctified Perception

Discernment is not just fact-checking. It is Spirit-formed perception. A sanctified way of seeing. It means asking not just, "Is this wrong?" but:

- Does this glorify Christ?
- Does this align with the full counsel of Scripture?
- Does this emphasize what God emphasizes?
- Is this building the Body—or branding the preacher?

It requires wisdom. And it requires humility. Because discernment is not about elevating self as the final arbiter of truth. It's about submitting all things to the One who is.

The Goal Is Not Exposure—It's Protection

Discernment is often weaponized for public takedown. That is not the biblical aim. The goal is not to expose people for clout. It is to protect truth, preserve the Church, and exalt Christ.

Discernment is a ministry of watchmen—those who guard the walls, protect the flock, and sound the alarm when subtle drift becomes dangerous theology.

Discernment should never be driven by ego. It must

always be driven by love for the Gospel and concern for the Church.

Spiritual Survival in the Age of Noise

In an age where every voice claims spiritual authority, discernment is not a luxury—it is survival.

- It's what keeps pulpits from becoming stages.
- It's what keeps teaching from becoming trend.
- It's what keeps Christ at the center instead of the speaker.

And it's what keeps the Church from "being tossed here and there by waves and carried about by every wind of doctrine, by the trickery of men, by craftiness in deceitful scheming" (Ephesians 4:14).

Reflection: Discernment Is Devotion

At its core, discernment is devotion.
It says:

"I love Your Word more than I love my favorite preacher's opinion."
"I trust Scripture more than I trust emotion."
"I follow Christ, not personalities."
"I want the real thing, even when it costs me comfort."

To discern is to love truth. To love truth is to love Christ. And to love Christ is to listen carefully, test constantly, and follow faithfully—even when the crowd moves in another direction.

Spotting the Near-Gospel

The greatest danger in today's Church is not the blatant lie—it's the almost-truth.

We know how to spot the obvious errors. We know to reject those who openly deny Christ, attack Scripture, or teach prosperity without repentance. But we are far less equipped to detect the half-truths—the ones that use Scripture's vocabulary but hollow out its meaning.

These messages don't shout heresy. They whisper distortion. They speak of love, but never mention sin. They proclaim grace, but remove the cross. They emphasize hope, but erase repentance. They offer transformation, but without dying to self. They carry the sound of truth, but lack the substance.

And because they are wrapped in familiarity, they go undetected by many.

The Anatomy of the Near-Gospel

The near-Gospel does not deny truth. It simply rearranges the emphasis. Christ is in the footnotes, man in the headlines. The cross is quoted—but not carried. Scripture is referenced—but only in fragments. It speaks of the kingdom without judgment, resurrection without crucifixion, grace without repentance.

Common phrases include:

"God wants you to flourish"—without "Take up your cross."
"You are enough—without "Christ alone is your righteousness."
"You are powerful"—without "When I am weak, then I am strong."

These messages aren't always false. They're unbalanced. And what's consistently omitted—repentance, submission, holiness—is what starves the soul.

A HOUSE DIVIDED

The Most Dangerous Sermons Aren't Always Wrong

Many of these sermons will not contain false statements. That's what makes them so persuasive.

They will affirm:

- God's love
- Human dignity
- The importance of community
- The healing nature of grace

But the danger isn't just in what is said—it's in what's consistently omitted. When sin is never mentioned, When repentance is never called for, When holiness is never pursued, When Scripture is used selectively, When Christ is treated as a motivational speaker instead of a crucified Savior—Then the Gospel has been gutted. It hasn't been denied. It's been replaced —slowly, subtly, and often unintentionally.

Discernment Isn't About Heresy-Hunting

Discernment is not about sniffing out error in every sermon. It is about knowing the real Gospel so deeply that anything less sounds hollow.

> *"My sheep hear my voice..."—John 10:27*

Counterfeit training in banks is not done by showing tellers fake money—it's done by letting them handle the real thing over and over again. That's how we prepare believers to recognize distortion.

- Let them be immersed in Scripture.
- Let them taste the richness of sound doctrine.

- Let them behold Christ—crucified, risen, and reigning.

Then, when a near-Gospel arrives, even in soft packaging, the center will feel off. The Gospel is not about affirmation. It's about redemption.

Ask the Right Questions

In a content-saturated age, we need filters stronger than emotion.
Ask:

1. What is this message emphasizing?
2. What is it consistently avoiding?
3. Does this message glorify Christ—or self?
4. Is this message shaped by Scripture—or by experience?
5. Is the tone convicting, comforting—or merely entertaining?
6. Does it stir me toward repentance—or only toward motivation?

Truth is not just what is said. It's what is centered.

The Gospel Does Not Flatter—It Frees

The Gospel is not flattering. It tells us we are dead in sin before it tells us we are alive in Christ. It demands crucifixion before resurrection. It offers rest, but after repentance. It speaks hope, but only to those who bow to its terms. The real Gospel humbles. It confronts. It wounds—then it heals. It does not cater to your potential. It kills your self-sufficiency. That's why the near-Gospel is so popular—it lets you keep your pride.

A HOUSE DIVIDED

What We Tolerate, We Will Eventually Teach

If we do not name the near-Gospel for what it is, we will pass it down as if it were whole.

- We will raise a generation that thinks comfort is a fruit of the Spirit.
- That conviction is toxic.
- That holiness is optional.
- That grace means permission, not transformation.

And we will wonder why the next generation walks away—not from Christ, but from the counterfeit we never exposed.

Reflection: Re-center the Cross

If a message does not:

- Begin at the cross
- Glorify the Son
- Submit to Scripture
- Produce holiness and lead to worship,

...it is not the Gospel. The real Gospel doesn't need marketing. It needs clarity. It needs to be lifted high. And it needs to be guarded fiercely. Because when near-truths are accepted, the true Gospel is diminished.

And when the Gospel is diminished, the power of salvation is diluted. Let us not settle for what sounds biblical. Let us contend for what is biblical—even when it is costly, offensive, or unpopular. Because it is only the true Gospel that saves.

One Voice. One Word. One Shepherd

In a noisy age, the Shepherd still speaks. He hasn't gone silent. He hasn't retreated behind complexity. He hasn't left His people without guidance. His voice remains. Steady. Clear. Scripture-rooted. Spirit-empowered.

But it is not loud in the way our world defines loud. It does not compete for attention like social content. It does not trend on emotion, nor shout above the latest controversy.

It speaks in alignment with His Word—and those who are near will hear it.

> *"My sheep hear My voice, and I know them, and they follow Me."—John 10:27*

That is the center of all discernment.

The Shepherd Still Speaks

In a generation overwhelmed by voices, it is crucial that we remember this: God has not stopped speaking. He has spoken definitively in His Son. He has preserved His truth in His Word. And He continues to guide His people through His Spirit.

But the world has changed. The noise has increased. And the Church has become accustomed to volume—as if that's what verifies authority. We gravitate toward what's prominent. We equate reach with revelation. We assume that if a voice is loud enough, it must be anointed. But the Shepherd does not compete with algorithmic volume. He speaks through Scriptural clarity.

Discernment Flows from Proximity, Not Platform

We don't need more content. We need more closeness. We don't need louder voices. We need deeper intimacy.

Discernment doesn't begin with theological categories. It begins with hearing the voice of the Shepherd in His Word.

It isn't about sniffing out every false teacher. It's about knowing the true Teacher so well that everything else fades. When you walk closely with Jesus— When you live with His Word open— When you let His Spirit search your motives— You develop not just a sharp mind, but a soft, trained heart.

That is the heart that discerns.

The Voice That Sanctifies

Jesus prayed in John 17:

> *"Sanctify them in the truth; your word is truth."*
> *—John 17:17*

The Word is not just information. It is transformation. And that transformation begins when we learn to submit to what He has already spoken. Discernment isn't simply about defending doctrine. It's about remaining set apart by truth in a world that weaponizes confusion.

We aren't sanctified by vibes. We aren't sanctified by influence. We aren't sanctified by popularity. We are sanctified by the Word—by hearing it, loving it, and living it.

The Disciple Learns the Shepherd's Tone

It's not just the content of His voice—it's the tone.

Jesus' voice is not abrasive. It's not manipulative. It's not flashy. It's not self-promoting. It is firm, yet tender. It wounds, then heals. It convicts without condemning. It calls without coercing. ...And once you learn that tone, other voices become easier to weigh.

The voice that constantly flatters you, without ever

confronting you, is not His. The voice that entertains but never leads you to holiness is not His. The voice that centers itself, and not the cross, is not His. But do not let discernment become distrust.

God has given the Church teachers, shepherds, and voices who speak with humility, consistency, and Scripture-saturated truth. Submit to such leaders—not blindly, but gratefully. True authority does not demand allegiance. It invites trust through a life aligned with the Word.

The Danger of Many Voices

There's nothing wrong with learning from many voices. But there's something very wrong with being formed by many voices without anchoring yourself to one Shepherd.

When every YouTube sermon becomes your authority, When every new influencer shapes your view of truth, When every post labeled "Christian" becomes food for your soul—Your spiritual palate becomes confused. Your ear becomes trained for noise, not truth. And then, when the Shepherd whispers—you may no longer recognize Him.

Intimacy as Protection

Discernment is not spiritual paranoia. It's not checking every statement with suspicion. It's not constantly fearing deception.

It's knowing your Shepherd so well that your heart is at rest in what He's already spoken. Proximity is protection. Not from suffering—but from seduction. Not from all error—but from following it blindly. Because when you are near to Christ, your spirit knows when something feels off. Even before you can name it intellectually, your heart resists it spiritually. This is not mystical. It is relational discernment. It is the fruit of walking with God.

We Don't Need More Noise—We Need More Nearness

The solution to spiritual confusion is not more noise. It is nearness to Christ. Nearness to His Word. Nearness to the Shepherd who gave His life for the sheep.

We need less commentary and more communion. Less spectacle and more Scripture. Less performance and more presence. Discernment is not a platform. It is a posture. It is not driven by ego. It is born in intimacy.

Reflection: Stay Close to the Shepherd

We are sheep in a digital wilderness. And in that wilderness, many voices will call our name. But only One voice leads to life.

> *"My sheep hear My voice, and I know them, and they follow Me."—John 10:27*

That's the invitation. That's the center of discernment. Not suspicion. Not tribalism. Not content fatigue. Proximity.

So if you want to discern—come closer. Turn down the noise. Open the Word. Stay with the Shepherd. Because when the Church listens again to one voice, under one Word, submitted to one Shepherd, clarity will return.

And so will power.

The Mirror of Betrayal

Some lessons are not learned through study. They are learned through ache. And among those, few are more clarifying—or more bitter—than betrayal. Personal betrayal sharpens discernment. Not automatically. Not instantly. But with time. With truth. With tearful endurance.

Betrayal reveals what discernment often misses: motives. It forces you to see who truly walked in truth—and who simply walked beside you for a season. It tears down assumptions. It exposes shadows. It does not just break trust. It breaks illusions.

The Gift No One Wants

Betrayal never arrives wrapped in wisdom. It comes cloaked in shock. In confusion. In the piercing contradiction of a face you trusted and the wound they caused. It shows up uninvited. It severs something sacred. And it often leaves the betrayed asking, "How did I not see it?"

The answer?

You weren't supposed to. God doesn't shame you for missing what others concealed. He uses it to deepen your sight, not to mock your past naivety, but to mature your discernment. In betrayal, charisma collapses. Gifting fades. Applause grows quiet. And character—true or false—stands exposed.

Not All That Glitters Is Faithful

In the modern Church, we've trained ourselves to equate presence with power. But betrayal reminds us: not all who walked with us were walking toward Christ.

- Some followed the light because it attracted a crowd.
- Some agreed with the truth because it benefited their image.

A HOUSE DIVIDED

- Some joined the mission, not because they believed it, but because they hoped to shape it.

And when their loyalty evaporates in the heat of conviction, we're left with this haunting truth: They never truly stood for what you stood for. They just stood near it—until truth required a cost.

Jesus Knows This Wound

> *"Even my close friend in whom I trusted, who ate my bread, has lifted his heel against me."*
> *—Psalm 41:9*

Jesus lived this psalm. He didn't just suffer for betrayal—He suffered through it. Judas wasn't an outsider. He wasn't a stranger. He was inside the circle, trusted with the finances, included in the miracles, named among the Twelve.

He kissed the face of Truth—and sold Him anyway. So when betrayal touches your life, you're not alone. You are being conformed to the path of the Savior who was betrayed by one He fed.

The Difference Between Who's With You and Who's For You

Betrayal teaches you to make a vital distinction: Not everyone who's with you is for you.

Some follow proximity. Some follow potential. Some follow momentum. But few will stay when truth divides, when obedience costs, or when faithfulness means staying instead of drifting. When they leave—or worse, when they wound you—don't mistake their departure for your failure. It's not a verdict against your worth. It's a revelation of their motives.

> *"They went out from us, but they were not of us..."*
> *—1 John 2:19*

The Mirror They Held Up

Betrayal is a mirror. But not of your faults. It reflects what the other person hid.

- Their insecurities
- Their hidden ambitions
- Their unspoken offense
- Their unrepentant ego

And yes, sometimes it reveals what you tolerated, hoping it would change. What you excused, thinking it was immaturity—not rebellion. What you loved, never knowing it would leave. But that mirror, as painful as it is, is also merciful. Because God will never let you build your obedience on illusion. Not forever.

Discernment Through the Ache

This is where betrayal becomes a teacher.

- It trains you to test fruit, not just charisma.
- It reminds you that consistency matters more than compliments.
- It deepens your love for truth—and your reluctance to chase applause.
- It sobers you toward your own assumptions.
- It helps you hear Christ's voice over the echo of public affirmation.

A HOUSE DIVIDED

You begin to measure people—not by how loud they cheer—but by how steady they walk. Not by what they post—but by what they practice. Not by how they flatter you—but by how they submit to Christ.

What Betrayal Refines

Let betrayal do its work—not to harden, but to hone:

- It will refine how you trust.
- It will refine what you listen for.
- It will refine your circle—not to isolate, but to insulate.
- It will protect your heart from being naïve again without making you cold.

Because what betrayal takes away in innocence, it gives back in sight. You don't just discern better theology. You begin to discern safe people. Humble leaders. True friends. Spiritual allies.

You Are Not Bitter—You Are Awake

There's a difference between bitterness and clarity. Bitterness holds grudges. Clarity releases—but remembers what God revealed. It doesn't mean you stay wounded. It means you stay watchful. It doesn't mean you stop trusting. It means you start testing. You can forgive and still say, "That person is not safe." You can move on and still carry the lesson that pain taught you. Forgiveness does not require blindness. In fact, it works best when your eyes are fully open.

Reflection: The Shepherd Over the Applause

At the end of betrayal's refining work is this gift: You trust the voice of Christ more than the applause of men.

You no longer chase crowds. You no longer confuse charisma with calling. You no longer accept loyalty without fruit. You no longer make peace with flattery at the expense of faithfulness. You walk slower. You listen more carefully. You lean into the Shepherd. Because His voice never betrayed you.

The Tide of Healing and the Return of Clarity

When Discernment Becomes Devotion, and Clarity Is Restored by Grace

Healing is not a moment. It's a tide. It ebbs and surges. It recedes, then returns. It whispers, then washes. And just when you think you've found your footing again, a memory pulls you back under—only for the next wave of grace to carry you a little further forward. This is the rhythm of restoration. Not linear. Not predictable. Not easily explained. But faithful. Holy. And sovereignly timed.

And for the watchman—who has walked through betrayal, confusion, and spiritual disillusionment—this tide is not a retreat from discernment. It is the fruit of it.

Discernment as the Doorway to Healing

Some assume that discernment is always aggressive—that to discern is to defend, to warn, to speak out, to stand apart. But there is another side. A quieter side. A devotional side.

Discernment, when shaped by the Spirit, doesn't just protect from error—it pulls us back to the Shepherd. It doesn't just guard the Gospel—it glorifies the One who gave it. It doesn't just confront the false. It heals what was fractured.

- Betrayal tore trust—but discernment reminded you that Jesus never changed.
- Confusion fogged your vision—but discernment re-centered you on the Word.
- Drift made your heart dull—but discernment drew you back to the voice that still speaks in clarity.

Healing begins not when the noise stops—but when you start listening again to the One voice that never lied to you.

You Are Not Defined by What Broke You

Many believers carry wounds they don't talk about—church wounds, leadership wounds, theological confusion, spiritual burnout.

These aren't scars from persecution. They are bruises left by the Body itself. You were told something was true, only to find out it was a preference. You were discipled into systems instead of into Christ. You were used instead of shepherded. You were hurt and then expected to stay silent "for the sake of unity."

So you drifted. Not because you stopped loving Jesus—but because you couldn't tell if anyone else still did. But that is not your ending. And it is not your identity.

> *"He restores my soul. He leads me in paths of righteousness for His name's sake."—Psalm 23:3*

You are not what was done to you. You are what He is doing in you now.

The Sting Fades. The Peace Returns.

One day, without planning for it, you realize something is different.

The sting is still remembered—but it no longer paralyzes. The face of betrayal still exists—but it no longer defines your prayers. The moment you lost your footing still matters—but now, your feet are on the Rock again.

And the noise? It's still there—but it no longer determines your direction. Because discernment has done its deeper work:

- It's not just sharpened your theology—it's softened your heart.
- It's not just exposed deception—it's restored your affection for Christ.

You don't hear Him with fear anymore. You hear Him with trust.

Discernment Wasn't Just for Defense—It Was for Devotion

We often think of discernment as a sword—wielded in battle. And it is. But it is also a lamp—guiding us home. Discernment is a scalpel in the hands of a surgeon. It cuts—but only to heal.

- It removes infection.
- It exposes what was buried.
- It sharpens what has grown dull.
- It separates bone from marrow, soul from spirit—not to shame, but to sanctify.

And what's left is not a hardened soul, but a holy one. A disciple who is no longer tossed by every wind of doctrine—but planted by the streams of living water. A worshiper who is no longer impressed by noise—but moved by the Word.

A HOUSE DIVIDED

You Know the Voice Now—And You Want to Stay Near It

> *"My sheep hear My voice, and I know them, and they follow Me."—John 10:27*

That is the outcome of holy discernment. Not paranoia. Not perfection. But proximity. Discernment that flows from pain—when surrendered to God—will lead not to pride, but to deeper intimacy with Christ.

You now know what His voice sounds like. And you know how to spot the counterfeit. You've seen what happens when the wrong people are followed. You've felt the ache of deception and the sting of trust misplaced.

And now?

You long for one thing: To stay close. To stay quiet before Him. To stay yielded. This is the clarity that healing brings.

Let the Tide of Grace Finish Its Work

Healing is not a finish line—it's a rhythm. Let grace pull you forward again.

- Forward from suspicion into spiritual confidence.
- Forward from grief into groundedness.
- Forward from pain into purpose.

The world does not need more spiritual commentators. It needs more wounded worshipers who know the cost of truth and the depth of mercy.

Discernment forged in trial becomes intercession. It becomes wisdom for others. It becomes a river of clarity for a confused Church.

Reflection: You Were Being Formed All Along

Discernment is not what saved you. But it's what kept you close.

It was never just about defending doctrine. It was about learning the voice of the Shepherd in the valley of shadows—and learning to love it more than the crowd's applause. That's what betrayal gave you. That's what healing restored. That's what clarity renewed. And now—truth doesn't just make you bold. It makes you devoted.

Watchman's Prayer

Lord, train my heart to hear Your voice above the crowd. Sharpen my eyes to see what is true, not just what is popular. Let me test the spirits—not with suspicion, but with Scripture. Make me bold, gentle, and awake.
In Jesus' name,
Amen.

7

The Faces That Oppose Truth

Understanding The Souls We Must Engage to Defend the Faith

Many Faces, One Burden

There are many faces in the fight for truth—but only one burden. Not every enemy of the Gospel looks like one. Some wear clerical collars. Others wear tears. Some shout. Others whisper. Some once sang in the choir. Others were never let in. But all of them—despite posture or tone—share this: they are souls. Not arguments. Not profiles. Souls.

In our zeal to defend truth, we've sometimes forgotten that.

We've argued with shadows, debated statistics, mocked caricatures. And in doing so, we've dulled our witness. Because we mistook spiritual resistance for intellectual rebellion. We mistook wounds for heresy. We tried to win the argument—and lost the person.

This chapter is not about winning. It's about seeing. It's about clarity without compromise, engagement without contempt. It's about burden—not irritation. Intercession—not indignation.

To be a Watchman is not merely to spot the enemy. It is to discern the soul behind the resistance. Not all opposition is rooted in arrogance. Some stems from abandonment. Others from confusion, disappointment, or spiritual distortion.

As apologists, our task is not merely to refute—but to reveal. Scripture calls us to contend for the faith (Jude 1:3), but also to answer "with meekness and fear" (1 Peter 3:15). Truth must be wielded like a sword—but held with trembling hands.

The world doesn't need louder defenders. It needs clearer ones. The Church doesn't need more polished rhetoric. It needs Watchmen who have wept.

Behind every argument—every denial, every "I'm spiritual, not religious"—is a soul with a wound or a worldview. That means behind every confrontation is an opportunity: to rightly divide the Word and rightly discern the person.

It's not enough to know doctrine. We must read the moment. We often assume rebellion where there is only confusion. We label heresy where there is hurt. And in doing so, we misrepresent the very truth we claim to defend.

This chapter introduces thirteen spiritual postures—not types, not categories. Patterns. Each one drawn from Scripture. Each one reflecting a unique challenge for the Watchman.

They are not psychological profiles. They are soul conditions.

You will meet the Wounded Skeptic, the Angry Deconstructionist, the Charismatic Deceiver, and others—each carrying not just resistance, but a story.

We cannot defend truth impersonally. The Gospel is not a talking point. It is a Person. And Christ didn't just answer arguments—He answered hearts.

He wept over Jerusalem. He warned Laodicea. He restored Peter. He rebuked Pharisees and comforted the outcast. His words were seasoned—but never soft. Pressing. Precise. Compassionate. Clear.

If we are to follow Him—not just in doctrine but in discernment—we must see resistance not merely as a threat, but as a test: of our posture, patience, and precision.

So let us begin. Not with suspicion, but with Scripture. Not to prove—but to plead. Not to label—but to love, even as we contend.

There are many faces. But only one burden. Truth spoken with compassion. Truth anchored in Christ. Truth that sees the soul.

Why People Resist Truth

Truth has never lacked power—but it has often lacked listeners.

From the beginning, resistance to truth has not been merely intellectual. It is a matter of the heart. And hearts, like soil, resist for different reasons. Some are hardened by pride. Others are choked by pain or distraction. Some are shallow. Others are strangled. But none are neutral.

This is the Watchman's burden: to realize that truth rejected is not always truth misunderstood. Sometimes it wounds before it heals. Sometimes it exposes what someone isn't ready to face.

Resistance isn't always loud. It may appear as avoidance, deflection, or even over-spirituality. It may wear the face of intellect, trauma, or culture. But beneath every argument lies a posture: a soul misaligned with the Word of God.

Jesus showed this in the parable of the soils (Matt. 13). The seed is the same. The sower is faithful. But the results differ—not because of the message, but because of the heart. The sower cannot change the soil. But he must know what kind he's dealing with.

Not all resistance is rebellion. Some is confusion. Some is fear. Some is deep disappointment.

We meet the Nicodemuses—curious, but cautious. The Thomases—honest, but hesitant. The Jonahs—resentful, not irreligious. And yes, the Judases—calculated, manipulative, dangerous.

Judas was not merely weak—he was willfully manipulative. His betrayal was calculated, cloaked in piety, and driven by agenda. Peter, by contrast, stumbled from fear—but was broken by it. He wept. He returned. The difference wasn't in the failure—it was in the response. One hardened. The other humbled. One clung to control. The other clung to Christ.

The Watchman must never confuse the two. Restoration is always possible—but only for the contrite. If we don't discern the difference, we'll reach for the wrong response. We'll use logic where we should offer love. Offer friendship where we should warn. And we'll confuse the bruised reed with the hidden wolf—healing one, enabling the other. That's why the Watchman must go beyond surface apologetics.

You are not just defending a system of doctrine. You are discerning soul conditions. And Scripture gives us the patterns: pride, fear, blindness, pain, manipulation, tradition, rebellion.

Paul told Timothy to correct "with meekness," in hopes that "God peradventure will give them repentance"

(2 Tim. 2:25). Repentance isn't generated by cleverness. It is granted by God—often through faithful discernment.

There is only one Gospel—but it lands on thirteen kinds of soil. Each requires a different posture from the Watchman. Because resistance is not always opposition. Sometimes it's an ache wearing armor. Sometimes it's sin hidden beneath style. And sometimes—it's war.

The Wounded Skeptic is bleeding—not rebelling.

The Intellectual may be hiding—behind logic, not arrogance.

The Apathetic Follower is forgetful—not forsaking.

The Overzealous Heretic may be afraid of grace—not malicious.

But we must not grow naïve.

The Charismatic Deceiver manipulates because we've exalted performance.

The Spiritual Manipulator is precise—like Judas, betraying with a kiss.

The Moral Relativist isn't just open-minded—he's defensive against truth.

The Cultural Conformist may not know he's bowed.

These are not quirks. They are soul diseases. And no disease is healed by cleverness alone. They must be confronted by the Word, through a vessel shaped by the Cross.

The Watchman must remember: we, too, once resisted. Maybe quietly. Maybe subtly. But we have all dodged the truth in some form. This is not neutrality. It is humility.

You must still defend. Still correct. Still call out deception. But never from pride. Always from mercy.

Why do people resist truth?

Because truth changes things. It dismantles pride. It demands repentance. It heals—but not without first cutting. And so, many hide in philosophies, personalities, or even spirituality. But the Watchman sees past the mask. He sees the posture. The wound behind the words. The story beneath the slogan. And because he sees—he speaks. Not just to expose. But to invite.

The Faces That Oppose

The Watchman does not debate profiles—he engages people. Each of these thirteen faces represents a posture of the soul, not just a personality trait. They are drawn from Scripture, shaped through the experiences of those who've walked the wall, and refined by the patterns God has already revealed. These are not psychological categories. They are spiritual conditions.

While these faces are described distinctly, they are not rigid compartments. A single soul may drift between categories—wounded and wandering, zealous and deceived, deconstructing yet still aching for justice. These postures often blur, overlap, or evolve. But naming them helps the Watchman discern where the Gospel must press, comfort, or confront.

The goal is not to reduce people to labels—but to recognize patterns that point to deeper needs. Some resist because they are proud. Others because they are pained. Some because they do not know the truth. Others because they fear what truth might cost them. But none are beyond God's reach.

Let the Watchman take note: these are not caricatures. They are not excuses to label or dismiss. They are invitations to discern, to intercede, to engage in a way that reflects the character of Christ and the authority of Scripture.

1. The Wounded Skeptic

Portrait: Once trusted. Now unsure. Their skepticism was born, not in rebellion, but in betrayal.
Biblical Parallel: The Samaritan Woman (John 4)
Watchman Engagement: Restore before you reason. Listen longer than you argue. Affirm dignity before offering doctrine. The heart must be heard before the Word is received.

2. The Intellectual

Portrait: Values logic, questions everything. Often more honest than hostile—but truth remains theoretical.
Biblical Parallel: Nicodemus (John 3); Athenians (Acts 17)
Watchman Engagement: Point to the Person, not just the premise. Build bridges through reason, but cross over into faith. Truth is not just a proposition—it's a Person.

3. The Angry Deconstructionist

Portrait: Once zealous. Now resentful. Their anger is often a cry against a system that failed them.
Biblical Parallel: Saul before conversion (Acts 8)
Watchman Engagement: Challenge their rage without mocking their pain. Let the light blind before it heals. What seems like rebellion may be unresolved betrayal.

4. The Charismatic Deceiver

Portrait: Performs well. Speaks in tongues. But manipulates through spiritual theatrics.
Biblical Parallel: Simon the Sorcerer (Acts 8); Jezebel (Rev. 2)
Watchman Engagement: Expose quietly, test boldly. Truth without showmanship reveals deception. Test the spirit—not just the sermon.

5. The Apathetic Follower

Portrait: Nods along but never moves. Spiritually numbed by distraction or routine.
Biblical Parallel: Laodicean Church (Rev. 3)
Watchman Engagement: Stir the soul, don't shame it. Offer a vision of holiness worth waking up for. The lukewarm need a holy fire.

6. The Moral Relativist

Portrait: Disguises doubt as open-mindedness. Defends ambiguity to avoid conviction.
Biblical Parallel: Pontius Pilate – "What is truth?" (John 18:38)
Watchman Engagement: Ground truth in reality. Reveal not just what is true—but what is unchanging. Don't just debate—disrupt their illusion of neutrality.

7. The Cultural Conformist

Portrait: Blends in. Adopts trends. Their faith is real—but buried beneath fear of man.
Biblical Parallel: Demas (2 Tim. 4:10); Israelites wanting a king (1 Sam. 8)
Watchman Engagement: Call them out by calling them up. Remind them who they are in Christ. Identity must rise before influence is resisted.

8. The Mystical Wanderer

Portrait: Loves spirituality, avoids Scripture. Seeks wonder, resists authority.
Biblical Parallel: Athenians with "new gods" (Acts 17); early Gnostics (1 John 4)
Watchman Engagement: Anchor their awe. Show them

that mystery finds its home not in vague energy—but in the incarnate Christ.

9. The Hurt Activist

Portrait: Zeal for justice. Anger toward the Church. Cries for truth, but burns bridges.
Biblical Parallel: Moses striking the rock (Num. 20); Jonah (Jonah 4)
Watchman Engagement: Redirect the flame. Validate the cry for justice, but guide it through grace. Anger can either consume—or confront rightly.

10. The Superficial Believer

Portrait: Christian in language, shallow in root. Follows Jesus until it costs something.
Biblical Parallel: John 6 crowd; rocky soil (Matt. 13:20–21)
Watchman Engagement: Invite to depth, not performance. Make the cost clear—and the joy deeper still. Discipleship demands decision.

11. The Overzealous Heretic

Portrait: Adds to the Gospel with passion. Loves doctrine, but lacks discernment.
Biblical Parallel: Judaizers in Galatia (Gal. 1–3); Peter's hypocrisy (Gal. 2)
Watchman Engagement: Re-center the Gospel. Correct publicly if needed—but restore privately when possible. Zeal must submit to grace.

12. The Silent Doubter

Portrait: Doesn't argue. Just fades. Doubt doesn't shout—it drifts into distance.

A HOUSE DIVIDED

Biblical Parallel: Thomas (John 20); John the Baptist (Matt. 11:3)
Watchman Engagement: Offer your scars. Invite honest questions. Let truth be touchable. Doubt is not deadly—unless we ignore it.

13. The Spiritual Manipulator

Portrait: Knows the lingo. Plays the part. Betrays while pretending to serve.
Biblical Parallel: Judas Iscariot; Ananias & Sapphira (Acts 5)
Watchman Engagement: Expose with clarity, protect the flock. Not all resistance is woundedness. Some is warfare. Truth must cut deeper than charisma.

This is the burden of the Watchman: to speak truth in love, but also in clarity. To confront spiritual conditions without cruelty—and to never confuse silence with safety.

Each of these faces stands between a lie and the truth. Some will turn. Some will fight. Some will fade. But all must be seen. And the Watchman who sees must also speak—not just with courage, but with discernment shaped by the Word of God.

Jesus and the Divided Crowd

He fed them—and they followed. But when He spoke truth, they walked away.

In John 6, after one of Jesus's most beloved miracles—the feeding of the five thousand—the people acknowledged His power and followed Him across the sea. But when He offered Himself as the Bread of Life, not just the source of bread, they turned back.

> *"From that time many of His disciples went back, and walked no more with Him."—John 6:66*

Jesus didn't soften His message to keep them. He didn't rebrand. He turned to the Twelve and asked, "Will ye also go away?"

This is the model of Christ-centered apologetics: truth offered not through pressure or manipulation, but invitation. The crowd had seen the signs. Their hunger was real—but misdirected. They wanted provision without surrender. So Jesus confronted their motives, offering words that thinned the crowd rather than pleased it. He spoke of eating His flesh and drinking His blood—not to confuse, but to expose. It separated those who wanted miracles from those who would follow through mystery. This is the chiastic center of the Watchman's call: Truth does not always gather—it divides.

We see the pattern again in John 8. When religious leaders drag a woman caught in adultery into Jesus' presence, He does not defend sin—but neither does He weaponize truth.

> *"He that is without sin among you, let him first cast a stone."—John 8:7*

He exposes both the woman's guilt and the crowd's hypocrisy. And then He turns to her, not with flattery, but mercy:

> *"Neither do I condemn thee: go, and sin no more."*
> *—John 8:11*

In both scenes, Jesus speaks with clarity—not compromise. With truth—not aggression. He tests the crowd by the Gospel, not the other way around. So must we.

A HOUSE DIVIDED

The Watchman must resist the urge to chase applause. The Church today is filled with crowds who want comfort, not correction—performance, not preaching. But Jesus never softened His words to retain numbers. He let them walk, and then turned to those who remained with truth, not triumph. That same question still echoes:

"Will you also go away?"

It confronts every sermon softened to avoid offense. Every silence in the face of deception. Every retreat into vagueness for the sake of keeping peace. Truth that thins the crowd is better than silence that multiplies it.

We do not speak to provoke—but neither do we retreat to preserve comfort. The Gospel Christ preached still confronts, divides, and invites. The faces we meet are not new. Some hunger but misunderstand. Some perform religion. Some are drowning in shame. Others are simply playing games.

The Watchman does not ask,

"What keeps them listening?"

He asks,

"What has God spoken?"

And he speaks it—whether the faces frown, walk, or stay.

How the Watchman Engages

It's one thing to recognize a soul's posture. It's another to respond like Christ. The Watchman doesn't stop at diagnosis—he engages with the discernment and mercy of Jesus. After confronting thirteen distinct faces of resistance, the temptation is to label and move on. But labels don't change lives. Love does. And truth spoken without love distorts the Gospel as much as silence does.

Jesus thinned crowds with hard truth—but He never mocked those who left. His tone was never cold. Every word He spoke, even in rebuke, carried both weight and redemptive purpose. He exposed deception, yes—but He wept for the deceived.

The Watchman must follow that pattern. Not all who resist are wolves. Some are sheep in pain. Others are wanderers. A few are pretenders. But all are souls Christ died to save. And the one who sees must also speak—not with superiority, but with sorrow-forged clarity. So what does this look like in practice? Here are the 13 faces—reframed not as categories, but as encounters.

1. The Wounded Skeptic

Then: Argues from pain. Distrusts easily.
Now: Listen more than lecture. Affirm their dignity before addressing their doubts. Truth feels safe when spoken by someone who sees the scar.

2. The Intellectual

Then: Hides behind logic. Fears surrender.
Now: Respect the mind, but reach for the soul. Ask what drives the questions—not just how to answer them. Truth is not just provable—it is personal.

3. The Angry Deconstructionist

Then: Demands justice. Burns bridges.
Now: Validate the ache without excusing the accusation. Let their rage be redirected by the cross—not silenced by counter-rants.

4. The Charismatic Deceiver

Then: Performs well. Manipulates softly.
Now: Test boldly. Confront cleanly. If deception harms others, expose it publicly. Never trade truth for talent.

5. The Apathetic Follower
Then: Spiritually sleepy. Nods along but never moves.
Now: Don't condemn—awaken. Preach the joy of costly obedience. Stir the soul with the beauty of holiness.

6. The Moral Relativist

Then: Defends ambiguity. Dodges conviction.
Now: Ground your words in reality. Truth is not flexible. Let clarity do the cutting—but speak with gentleness.

7. The Cultural Conformist

Then: Fears rejection. Faith hidden behind approval.
Now: Call them to courage. Remind them whose name they bear. Identity must be reclaimed before influence can be resisted.

8. The Mystical Wanderer

Then: Loves mystery. Resists Scripture.
Now: Anchor awe in Christ. Show that wonder finds its fullness in the Incarnation—not in energy or experience.

9. The Hurt Activist

Then: Zealous, but untethered.
Now: Honor the cry for justice—but align it with the justice of the cross. Anger can confront rightly when discipled.

10. The Superficial Believer

Then: Christian by label. Shallow in root.
Now: Preach cost and joy together. Don't flatter—invite to depth. Jesus never promised ease. He promised resurrection after the cross.

11. The Overzealous Heretic

Then: Passionate. Misguided.
Now: Correct with clarity—and restore with humility. Don't mock their zeal. Redirect it with Gospel grace.

12. The Silent Doubter

Then: Quiet. Drifting.
Now: Pursue them. Ask what no one else is asking. Let them see your scars. Offer a space where doubt can wrestle with truth.

13. The Spiritual Manipulator

Then: Plays the part. Destroys trust.
Now: Protect the flock. Expose deceit. If they repent, restore with caution. If not, guard the gate.

The Watchman is not just a messenger of truth. He is a vessel of mercy.

Gospel Vision: What Every Face Needs

Each soul posture—whether hardened, hesitant, or hiding—still needs the same Christ.

- The Wounded need healing through mercy, not avoidance
- The Proud need humbling grace, not intellectual conquest

- The Confused need clarity tethered to compassion
- The Deceived need truth that both exposes and restores
- The Passive need vision that awakens purpose
- The Zealous but Misled need Gospel re-centering, not ridicule

The Gospel does not flatter. It does not cater. It does not edit to win approval. It calls every face—every soul—to the same place:

The Cross. There, pride is broken. Wounds are bound. Doubt is confronted. Sin is named. And grace is not vague—it is victorious. Let the Watchman lead souls there—one burdened truth at a time. These faces are not "them"—they are us, too.

We have all doubted. We have softened truth. We have resisted surrender. And so, we do not speak down to these souls. We speak across—with the humility of those who have been rescued, too.

The Watchman's goal is not conquest—it is conversion. Not triumph in debate—but transformation in Christ. To engage is not to win—it is to witness.

What the Gospel Demands of Us

We've named the faces. We've traced the soul-postures that resist truth. But now comes the harder question: What does the Gospel demand of the one who sees them?

The danger is not just in their deception—it's in our drift. The Watchman's task is not to diagnose from a distance. It is to stand close enough to weep. Precision without compassion is not faithfulness—it's failure. If we expose error but grow cold in the process, we've abandoned the Spirit who gave us truth in the first place.

Jesus faced crowds of liars, legalists, and manipulators. But He didn't just expose them—He bore their sin. Paul rebuked churches—but did so like a father in labor.

Stephen, as he was stoned, prayed for his murderers. This is our call: clarity without cruelty. Courage without contempt. Burden without bitterness. We are not defenders of doctrine alone. We are bearers of mercy.

And every one of the 13 faces is a soul Christ died for. So what does that mean for us?

1. Grieved Clarity

Not every confrontation should feel like a debate. Some should feel like a funeral. If we see error without sorrow, we are not qualified to speak. It was grace, not brilliance, that opened our eyes. Let that grace season every word we speak.

2. Courageous Consistency

Do not dilute truth to preserve peace. Do not edit Scripture to protect influence. Jesus let crowds leave. Paul lost friends. Elijah stood alone. Jeremiah wept in prison. Stephen died preaching. But none of them changed the message.

You are not responsible for the results—only for your faithfulness.

3. Burdened Intercession

We do not just argue with people—we must pray for them. Jesus prayed for Peter before the denial. Paul wept for Israel daily. Real burden bends the knees.

Do you intercede for the deconstructing—or do you just collect rebuttals? Watchmen who don't pray will speak with no power. Apologists who don't grieve will mock what they're called to reach.

4. Repentant Humility

This isn't just a lens to examine others. It's a mirror. If you saw the 13 faces and never saw yourself—you missed the point. We've all softened truth. We've all resisted obedience. Maybe yours was cloaked in ministry success. Or buried in theological pride. But it was resistance nonetheless. And the Gospel calls us to repent—again and again. The Watchman is not above the people he warns. He's simply awake.

5. Gospel-Fueled Vision

Truth isn't just to be defended—it's to be delivered. You don't need brilliance. You need fidelity.

This means:

- Speak boldly, even if misunderstood.
- Correct gently, even if mocked.
- Warn fiercely, even if ignored.
- And keep standing—even if they walk away.

Because Christ stood for you. Because He still bears with you. The Gospel does not require your perfection—but it does require your participation. Not in platform-building, but in burden-bearing. If you carry this truth, then carry the Cross that comes with it.

Watchman's Prayer

Lord, teach me to see past the argument and into the soul. Give me discernment not just for doctrines, but for people.

JUEL MENDEZ

Let me speak clearly, love boldly, and stand humbly. And may I never forget: the face that opposes today may be the friend who follows tomorrow.

In Jesus' name,
Amen

8

A Kingdom Without Walls

Building Bridges Through Shared Essentials

Brick by Brick or Wall by Wall?

Imagine a city under construction. Each builder arrives with bricks—some red, some gray, some chipped, some smooth. Each shaped by conviction, marked by tradition, and worn by experience. Some are heavy with history. Others fresh from revival. In the hands of a wise builder, each has a place.

At first, it seems the builders are united. They speak of foundations. Blueprints. The glory to come. The first stones are laid with shared hope and joy.

But something shifts.

Instead of placing their bricks side by side—interlocking them into one structure—they begin stacking them into isolated towers. The work halts. The vision

A HOUSE DIVIDED

fragments. The city of God becomes a grid of fortified camps.

Walls rise where doorways were meant to be. Each group defends its section with zeal. Flags go up. Names are etched in stone. Creeds become codes. Distinctives become dividing lines. The mortar of humility dries—and the shouting begins. From behind these self-made walls, they hurl warnings:

"You don't preach like us."
"You don't worship like us."
"You don't baptize like us."
"You're not really part of the Church—not like we are."

This is what has happened to the Body of Christ.

A Kingdom Divided

Denominations were never the enemy. Many were born in the fires of reform and awakening. They were meant to clarify truth, sharpen theology, and steward distinctives. But over time, what began as an effort to define the Gospel became a system for dividing the saints.

Creeds and confessions—originally crafted to guard the Gospel—are now often used as border checkpoints. We no longer ask, "Do you believe the Gospel of Jesus Christ, crucified and risen?"

We ask:

"Do you line up with our view of election?"
"Do you read Revelation our way?"
"Do you use wine or grape juice? Raise hands or fold them? Speak in tongues or avoid it altogether?"

The early Church was built stone upon stone, each life joined together into a holy temple, with Christ as the cornerstone. But we've taken our favorite stones and built walls around them. Walls to keep others out. Walls to showcase our brand of fidelity. Walls to protect our tribe more than to proclaim the truth.

A Shattered Skyline

The result?
 The world doesn't see one temple rising in unity. It sees a fractured skyline of theological towers. A splintered silhouette of division. It doesn't hear one Gospel. It hears competing broadcasts—each with subtle differences in tone, emphasis, and boundary lines. It doesn't see one Body. It sees a house divided—and turns away. To the watching world, we often resemble rival corporations:

- Each claiming to offer the real product, each distrusting the next, each marketing its own theological brand with sleek packaging and quiet disclaimers.

This is not what Christ prayed for. This is not what the apostles died for. This is not what the Spirit empowered the Church to become.

Jesus Didn't Build Towers—He Built Tables

The Kingdom Christ came to build has no moat, no spotlighted towers, no locked gates. It has a cross-shaped doorway—open to all who believe. He did not say,

> "Make walls of doctrine and guard them with suspicion."

He said,

A HOUSE DIVIDED

> *"Make disciples of all nations."—Matthew 28:19*

He didn't say,

> *"Be right in all things."*

He said,

> *"Be one as We are one."—John 17:21*

He didn't gather twelve disciples to start twelve ministries. He broke bread. He washed feet. He tore down the systems that divided Jew and Gentile, male and female, slave and free.

He welcomed the doubter, the zealot, the tax collector, and the outcast—and made them one Body.

We Are Called to Rebuild—Not Fortify

The call of the Church is not to fortify our sections, but to rebuild the house.

We are not called to echo our traditions. We are called to embody Christ. And Christ does not build with tribal loyalty. He builds with living stones—people transformed by grace, rooted in the Gospel, filled with the Spirit, and joined together as one. Not by uniformity, but by unity. Not by identical methods, but by shared allegiance. Not by systematic agreement, but by Gospel surrender.

From Barriers to Bridges

The walls must fall. Not the walls of truth—but the walls of pride. Not the guardrails of doctrine—but the gates of division.

We must become bridge builders, not tribal sentinels. People who know how to hold to conviction without crushing communion. People who value truth without vilifying those who differ on secondary matters. People who welcome fellowship not based on theological exactitude—but on shared redemption.

If Christ is the cornerstone, we cannot keep building walls in His name. If the blood of Jesus unites us, nothing else should divide us. If the Gospel is our common ground, then let us build the Kingdom together—brick by brick, not wall by wall.

Unity Flourishes Around Shared Essentials, Not Forced Uniformity

Unity in the Body of Christ does not begin with systems. It begins with surrender. Not surrender to a denomination, a movement, or a theological tribe—but to Christ. To the Gospel. To the finished work of the cross and the full authority of Scripture.

Unity that is forced is not unity at all. It is uniformity—an external agreement imposed by pressure or fear. But the unity Jesus prayed for in John 17 was not a conformity of form—it was a communion of Spirit.

It was a unity that did not flatten differences—but lifted Christ above them.

The Unity of the Early Church Was Never Based on Sameness

The early Church was a mosaic. Jew and Gentile. Greek and Hebrew. Pharisee and fisherman. Servants and scholars. Poor and powerful. Soldiers and slaves.

They did not agree on everything.

- Some kept the Sabbath.
- Some ate meat sacrificed to idols.
- Some observed Jewish festivals.
- Others rejected them as obsolete.

A HOUSE DIVIDED

But Paul does not demand uniformity in all things. He demands humility in all things—and unity in the essentials.

> *"Accept the one whose faith is weak, without quarreling over disputable matters."*
> —Romans 14:1

Disputable matters. Not unimportant—but not ultimate. Not dismissible—but not divisive. But how do we know when to separate—and when to bear with?

Scripture offers a framework. Heresy denies the essentials of the Gospel: the nature of God, the person and work of Christ, salvation by grace through faith, and the authority of Scripture. When these are compromised, unity is broken at the foundation—and separation may be necessary (Gal. 1:8–9; 2 John 10).

But when believers differ on disputable matters—those not central to salvation—Romans 14 calls us to bear with one another in love. We do not affirm all views as equally true, but we distinguish between error and destruction, between disagreement and denial of the faith.

Fidelity does not always mean separation. Sometimes it means staying—to teach, to love, to sharpen. And that requires wisdom formed by Scripture, not fear.

Essentials Are the Bedrock. Everything Else Is Scaffold.

We must learn to distinguish between foundational truths and structural distinctives.

There are certain doctrines we must never negotiate. These are the immovable stones at the center of Christian unity:

- The Trinity: One God, three persons—Father, Son, and Holy Spirit.

- The full deity and humanity of Jesus: God in flesh, the incarnate Son.
- The authority and inspiration of Scripture: God's Word, sufficient and trustworthy.
- Salvation by grace through faith: Not by works, not by ritual, but by faith in Christ alone.
- The bodily resurrection of Jesus: The risen Christ, victorious over sin and death.

These are the non-negotiables of the faith. The guardrails of Gospel fellowship. These essentials are not innovations—they are affirmations of the ancient faith once delivered to the saints. The early Church guarded them through creeds that still echo across centuries: the Apostles' Creed, the Nicene Creed, the Chalcedonian Definition.

These were not tribal slogans. They were theological anchors—crafted not to divide believers, but to unite them around the unchanging Gospel. They remind us: Christian unity is not new. It is rooted in the earliest declarations of who Christ is and what He has done. The truths for which we must contend—even if it costs us everything.

But beyond these?

The scaffolding differs. And we must be careful not to mistake our scaffolding for the cornerstone.

Unity Is Not Sameness. It's Surrender to the Same Savior.

We can disagree on the mode of baptism—and still baptize in Christ. We can differ on the gifts of the Spirit—and still walk by the same Spirit. We can attend different styles of worship—while lifting the same Jesus. We can read Revelation differently—while proclaiming the same coming King.

If we agree on the Gospel, we are family. This does

not mean all differences disappear. It means they are held in their proper place. In the essentials: unity. In the non-essentials: liberty. In all things: charity. This is not theological compromise. It is theological maturity.

Fellowship Should Not Depend on Perfect Alignment

Imagine refusing to labor in evangelism with another believer because they hold a different view of church governance. Or refusing to share communion because their eschatology doesn't match yours. Or dismissing a powerful book because its author was baptized differently than you. This is not discernment. It is division disguised as purity.

Paul warned the Galatians against adding requirements to the Gospel (Galatians 1). And yet we often add so many fences to our fellowships that the cross becomes inaccessible to those just steps away.

It is one thing to separate from false gospels. It is another thing entirely to separate from faithful brothers and sisters who do not pronounce every syllable of doctrine like we do.

Truth Must Remain—But Love Must Flow

We must not lower the standard of truth. But we must raise the standard of love. Unity is not the absence of disagreement. It is the presence of Christ above all. It's how we disagree that reveals whether we are truly one Body.

Do we attack? Or do we appeal? Do we correct? Or do we cancel? Do we tear down? Or do we come alongside?

> *"By this all men will know that you are my disciples,*
> *if you have love for one another."—John 13:35*

Our divisions have not only weakened our witness. They have distorted our message. Because a divided Church cannot proclaim a reconciling Christ.

The Watchman's Balance: Grace and Gravity

To contend for the faith is not to crush everyone who differs. It is to hold fast the Gospel with grace and gravity.

- Grace for the honest struggler, the slow learner, the well-meaning brother in error.
- Gravity when truth is distorted, when essentials are attacked, when wolves enter the flock.

This is not compromise. It is discernment. It is knowing when to break fellowship—and when to bear with the weak. It is knowing the difference between a deceiver and a disciple who still needs to grow.

The Watchman does not ignore falsehood. But neither does he fire arrows at fellow soldiers because they wear different armor.

Unity Must Be Built on the Right Foundation

We are not one because we agree on everything. We are one because we are all held together by Christ. Unity is not maintained by checking boxes. It is maintained by crucifying pride. By walking in humility. By striving for the bond of peace. The Gospel is enough to unite us. Christ is enough to hold us. The Spirit is enough to teach us.

So let us lay down the need for sameness. And take up the call to walk side by side—under the blood, by the Spirit, for the Name.

The Sectarian Spirit

A HOUSE DIVIDED

Sectarianism is not merely division—it is pride baptized in theological language. It is what happens when a Church forgets that it was saved by grace, and begins to act as though it was saved by alignment.

It is not just disagreement. The Church has always had disagreement. The Jerusalem Council in Acts 15. The debates in Romans 14. The confrontations in Galatians 2.

The problem is not differing convictions. The problem is when those convictions become weapons—used not to sharpen, but to sever. Used not to protect the Gospel—but to elevate the tribe.

Tribe Over Truth

Sectarianism is what happens when we stop asking,

> *"What does the Word say?"*

And start asking,

> *"What does our group say?"*

- A church refuses to join in evangelism because the other church uses guitars.
- A pastor refuses fellowship because the other doesn't affirm all five points of Calvinism.
- A ministry declines to endorse a helpful book because its author belongs to a different denomination.

None of these actions are based on heresy. They are rooted in preference. Pride. Positioning. And they are often dressed in the language of faithfulness:

> *"We're just being discerning."*
> *"We must guard the truth."*

"We don't want to confuse our people."

But underneath the language is a fear of proximity. A fear that being near another part of the Body will somehow stain our own. As if fellowship were a threat to truth. As if Christ were divided.

Paul Saw This Spirit—and Confronted It Head-On

The Corinthian church had turned spiritual leaders into camps.

> *"Each of you says, 'I follow Paul,' or 'I follow Apollos,' or 'I follow Cephas,' or 'I follow Christ.'"*
> *—1 Corinthians 1:12*

To modern ears, it sounds like this:

> *"I follow Reformed theology."*
> *"I follow Charismatic fire."*
> *"I follow ancient liturgy."*
> *"I follow the New Testament church model."*

On the surface, these may be expressions of devotion. But when they become dividing lines—when they become more central than the Gospel itself—they become sectarian. And Paul's response is thunderous:

> *"Is Christ divided?"—1 Corinthians 1:13*

This is not a rhetorical question. It is a rebuke. Because when we divide the Body over secondary identities, we are functionally denying the unity that Christ has already accomplished. We may not say it aloud. But our behavior says it for us:

"Jesus is enough for salvation—but not enough for fellowship."

A HOUSE DIVIDED

Modern Sectarianism Wears Stylish Robes

It is subtle. It is polite. It is often applauded in the echo chambers of our tribe. It says:

> "We don't associate with those who use different translations."
> "We won't share communion unless your church governance matches ours."
> "We can't invite her to speak—she believes in spiritual gifts."

Again, the issue here is not truth. It is elevation. It is when tertiary truths become territorial flags. When distinctions become divisions. When convictions become ultimatums. And we begin to define ourselves not by what we believe—but by who we exclude.

Sectarianism Is Not Fidelity to the Gospel. It Is a Denial of It.

It creates pride where there should be poverty of spirit. It builds fences where Christ built a family. It glorifies systems, labels, camps, and tribes—until they sit higher than the Gospel itself.

You can be doctrinally precise and spiritually sectarian. You can be biblically literate and still build walls Christ came to tear down. The Pharisees knew the Scriptures. But they crucified the Word made flesh. Let us not make the same mistake.

When Loyalty to the Tribe Outweighs Love for the Body

If your deepest loyalty is to a confession instead of Christ, If your first test of fellowship is tribal alignment instead of Gospel allegiance, If your instinct is to withdraw before you ask what unites— You may be operating under a sectarian spirit. And here's the tragedy: The world sees it. The next generation sees it. They hear our debates. They feel our disdain. And they wonder if the Church really believes the love it preaches. Because what we tolerate in tone eventually becomes what we teach in truth. If we model suspicion, others will inherit division.

Reforming the Reformers

You can love your theological heritage and still repent of its excesses. You can honor the tradition that shaped you without making it the standard for everyone else. You can say:

> *"I'm Reformed, but not superior."*
> *"I'm Baptist, but open-handed."*
> *"I'm Charismatic, but grounded."*
> *"I'm liturgical, but loving."*
> *"I'm not ashamed of my distinctives—but I refuse to make them my identity."*

Because our identity is not found in the movement we follow. It is found in the Messiah who found us.

What the Church Needs Now

The Church needs more bridge-builders than brand ambassadors. More foot-washers than flag-bearers. More pastors who say,

> *"Let's reason together,"*

instead of,

> *"You don't belong."*

It needs Watchmen who see beyond the wall. Who call for unity—not by flattening truth—but by lifting

Christ higher than every banner. It needs grace that listens. Truth that loves. Courage that embraces the Body in all its complexity. Because the Gospel is bigger than our tribe. And Christ is not divided.

Ephesians 2–4 and the Tearing Down of Walls

The divisions we see in the Church today are not new. They may have new names, new creeds, new labels—but their root is ancient.

In the first century, the divide was clear and cultural: Jew and Gentile. Two worlds. Two histories. Two interpretations of righteousness. One chosen nation. One adopted people. One Messiah—misunderstood by both. But in Christ, the wall between them was not negotiated. It was demolished. And Paul, writing from prison, puts it in terms so vivid, so final, that no amount of theological tribalism can safely ignore it.

He Himself Is Our Peace

> *"For He Himself is our peace, who has made us both one and has broken down in His flesh the dividing wall of hostility..."—Ephesians 2:14*

This is not poetic language. It is a spiritual reality. A declaration of cosmic reconstruction.

Jesus didn't merely reconcile sinners to God. He reconciled them to each other. Jew and Gentile. Law-keepers and lawless. Clean and unclean. He brought them together not by ignoring their differences—but by subordinating them to the cross.

And how did He do it?

Not through negotiation. Not through theological

roundtables. But through His own body—broken, bruised, crucified. He tore down the wall of hostility by absorbing the hostility Himself. The wall did not fall gently. It fell on Him.

A New Humanity in Christ

Paul goes on:

> *"...that He might create in Himself one new man in place of the two, so making peace, and might reconcile us both to God in one body through the cross..."—Ephesians 2:15-16*

This is not unity by compromise. It is unity by crucifixion. Christ didn't come to make Gentiles more Jewish, or Jews more Greek. He came to make a new kind of person—a new creation, born of grace, bound by the Spirit. One body. One people. One household. Not uniform, but indivisible. Not identical, but inseparable.

Paul says we are no longer strangers and aliens. We are citizens. We are family. We are stones in the same temple. Walls don't belong in families. They don't belong in temples. And they don't belong in the Church.

Keep the Unity Already Purchased

Many think unity is something we must create. But Paul corrects this.

> *"Make every effort to keep the unity of the Spirit through the bond of peace."—Ephesians 4:3*

We do not create unity. Christ already did.
Our job is to keep it. Protect it. Guard it. To resist

A HOUSE DIVIDED

the pull of suspicion and tribalism. To walk worthy of the calling we've received—not just in moral purity, but in relational humility.

How do we keep that unity?

Paul tells us:

> *"With all humility and gentleness, with patience, bearing with one another in love."*
> —*Ephesians 4:2*

This is where unity lives: Not in uniformity of method, but in mutual submission. Not in agreement on all things, but in surrender to Christ in all things. Unity is fragile not because truth is weak—but because pride is strong.

Walls We Rebuild Today

Jesus tore down the wall. But we keep rebuilding it. We stack it back up with denominational suspicion. We reinforce it with tribal loyalty. We guard it with theological pride. We call it "faithfulness," but it's often just fear. Fear of being misunderstood. Fear of contamination. Fear of loss of control.

We pretend our differences must equal distance. We behave as if theological fences are the same as spiritual walls. But they are not.

Some fences are necessary—to guard the sheep, to mark off heresy, to preserve Gospel clarity. But many of our fences have become fortresses. And fortresses do not foster family. They foster factions.

Peace Is Not the Absence of Conflict—It's the Presence of Christ

The peace that Christ brings is not passive. It's not

tolerance. It's not avoidance. It's not fake smiles in public and suspicion in private. It is a peace born of the blood of the cross. A peace that:

- Calls us to lay down our swords
- Invites us to sit at the same table
- Commands us to forgive as we've been forgiven
- Demands we stop measuring others by our camp, and start seeing them in Christ

This is not optional. It is the outworking of the Gospel. Because the Gospel that reconciles us to God cannot leave us unreconciled to each other.

Let the Walls Fall Again

If Christ broke down the wall in His flesh, why are we rebuilding it with our traditions? If the Spirit sealed us into one Body, why do we act as if our section is the only one worth defending? If the Father adopted us into one household, why do we keep drawing boundary lines through the living room? The call of Ephesians is not vague ecumenism. It is Gospel-fueled reconciliation. It is truth with tears. It is doctrine with love. It is grace with gravity.

Watchman's Call

The Watchman sees what others dismiss. He does not just guard against error. He guards the unity Jesus died to give. He stands on the wall not to divide the Church—but to remind her she is one. He watches for wolves. But he also watches for wedges. And when he sees the wall going up again—brick by brick, tribe by tribe—he sounds the alarm. Not to shame the builders. But to remind them:

- The cornerstone is Christ.

- The foundation is the apostles. A
- And the temple we are building cannot afford to be divided.

Let the walls fall again.

Kingdom Citizens Before Denominational Members

It is not wrong to be Baptist. Or Presbyterian. Or Pentecostal. It is not wrong to belong to a tradition, to find clarity in a confession, or to learn from a particular stream of the Church's long, faithful witness. But it is dangerous when that identity becomes ultimate.

When we lead with tribe instead of truth. When we introduce our theology before we declare our Savior. When we defend our camp more than we defend the Gospel. We were never meant to find our deepest identity in our denominational label. We were meant to find it in our citizenship in a Kingdom not made with human hands. This does not mean denominations have no value.

In fact, God has often used them—flawed as they are—to advance the Gospel. Through them, Bibles have been translated, missionaries sent, schools built, revivals sparked, and churches planted in every corner of the earth. The danger is not in structure—but in supremacy. When our denomination becomes the lens through which we see every other believer, we've lost the global, eternal scope of the Kingdom.

The Cross Came Before the Council

Before there were synods, sessions, bishops, or boards—there was blood. Christ did not die to found a tradition. He died to redeem a people. A people not bound by polity or style, but by Spirit. A people called from every tribe, every tongue, every denomination and non-denomination.

The early Church had no denominations. It had elders. Apostles. Disciples. Servants. Brothers and sisters. Their unity wasn't based on structural sameness—it was based on shared salvation. They were first and foremost citizens of Heaven (Philippians 3:20). That was their banner. That was their burden.

Denominational Labels Must Serve the Gospel—Not Supplant It

Denominations can be useful. They give structure. They preserve heritage. They can help believers walk in clarity. But when those labels start functioning as lines of spiritual worth—When our theological family tree becomes a fence rather than a framework—We've crossed from biblical fidelity into sectarian pride. We must stop leading with:

> *"I'm Reformed."*
> *"I'm Wesleyan."*
> *"I'm Charismatic."*
> *"I'm non-denominational."*
> *"I'm conservative."*
> *"I'm traditional."*

And start leading with:

> *"I belong to Jesus."*
> *"I've been crucified with Christ."*
> *"I am not my own—I've been bought with a price."*

When our identity in Christ is eclipsed by our loyalty to a tradition, we are no longer contending for the faith—we are campaigning for a flag.

What Do We Actually Preach?

A HOUSE DIVIDED

Ask yourself: when people hear you speak about the Church, what do they hear more of?

- Do they hear the Gospel of Christ, or the distinctives of your theological system?
- Do they walk away knowing Jesus is supreme—or that your camp is sound?
- Do they feel invited to the cross—or pressured into conformity?

We must proclaim truth boldly. But the truth must always flow from the Person and work of Christ—not the pedigree of our label. You can be faithful to Scripture without being tribal. You can love your confession without making it your confession of faith.

Rebuild Fellowship by Remembering the Cross

If we are to walk as citizens of the same Kingdom, then we must learn how to hold one another in grace, not just agreement.

Here's how we rebuild true fellowship:

- Focus on shared essentials. The deity of Christ. His atoning work. His resurrection. The authority of Scripture. Salvation by grace. If we agree here, we stand on the same ground.
- Honor one another's convictions. Not dismissively. Not silently. But with understanding and humility. You don't have to agree with everything to respect someone's faithfulness.
- Differentiate between error and difference. Not every disagreement is heresy. Not every secondary issue is a threat to orthodoxy. We must learn to distinguish the two.

This doesn't mean we pretend our convictions don't matter. It means we treat people like they matter more.

Disciples First, Denominations Second

If a brother in Christ affirms the Gospel, walks in repentance, submits to the authority of Scripture, and seeks to glorify God—then that brother is family. Even if his worship looks different. Even if his polity is structured differently. Even if his reading of Revelation takes a different route.

We must stop drawing battle lines where Jesus has drawn bloodlines. Because when we divide over preferences and elevate distinctions to the level of doctrine, we blur the very Gospel we're called to proclaim.

Jesus Didn't Die for a Denomination

Jesus didn't die to preserve Calvinism. Or Arminianism. Or liturgy. Or charismatic expressions. Or high church or low church. He died to reconcile sinners to God and to one another. He died to break down walls, not build new ones. He died to create one flock under one Shepherd. If our theology doesn't lead us to love other Gospel-believers more deeply, it's not Gospel-shaped theology. If our doctrine makes us more suspicious than sacrificial, it's not modeled after Christ. If our banner causes us to ignore the rest of the Body, we're waving the wrong flag.

The Badge of the Kingdom Is Not a Brand—It's a Cross

We are marked, not by logos or language, but by the Spirit of the living God. Our loyalty is not to systems—but to the Savior. Not to tribes—but to truth. Not to confessions first—but to the crucified Christ. We are citizens of a Kingdom that will outlast every theological tribe. We are brothers and sisters of a family that no denomination owns. We are members of a Body whose Head is Christ—not a founder, not a movement, not a network.

Watchman's Reflection

If you are a Watchman on the wall, you must see beyond your camp. You must warn against wolves—but also rebuke walls. You must test the spirits—but also test your pride. You must guard the truth—but never confuse truth with tribal loyalty. Be a Kingdom citizen before anything else. And help others do the same. Because only one banner will fly in glory. And it will not bear your denominational label. It will bear the name of Jesus Christ, risen and reigning.

Confessional Walls, Gospel Bridges

Confessions matter. They are the theological backbone of many faithful churches and movements. They clarify convictions. They anchor us in orthodoxy. They guard against doctrinal drift.

They represent the hard-won wisdom of generations who sought to faithfully interpret the Word of God. But like any good thing, confessions become dangerous when misused.

They are meant to be guardrails, not gates. They are meant to preserve unity in truth—not fracture unity in Christ. They are meant to protect the Gospel—not replace it. The danger is subtle: when what was meant to serve the Gospel becomes something we substitute for the Gospel. And that is when a confession becomes a wall.

Walls Built with Good Intentions

No one sets out to build barriers with their statement of

faith. Most walls begin as lines. Necessary lines. Doctrinal clarity lines. Boundary lines. But when we start treating those lines as boundary markers for salvation—or as tests of full fellowship—something shifts.

What began as a confession becomes a checklist. What was once a tool becomes a test. What started as clarity becomes control. And suddenly, the Church is no longer seen as one body. It is seen as clusters of competing camps—each with its own entry code.

But Jesus didn't say,

"You will know them by their alignment with your statement of faith."

He said,

"By this all men will know that you are my disciples—if you have love for one another."
—*John 13:35*

A Gospel Bridge Is Stronger Than a Confessional Wall

The Gospel is the bridge that holds the Body together. Not just for sinners to cross into salvation—but for saints to walk toward each other in humility.

It is the message that:

- Unites Jew and Gentile
- Reconciles Peter and Paul
- Includes the thief on the cross and the scholar in the synagogue
- Gathers the early Church under persecution and the global Church under one Savior

This Gospel is bigger than your confession. It is

older than your tradition. It is wider than your camp. And it is stronger than the theological bricks we stack between us. Because while confessions are human words about truth, the Gospel is the truth.

We Do Not Tear Down Truth—We Tear Down Pride

Let this be clear: we do not tear down the walls that guard against heresy. We do not remove the fences that mark orthodoxy. We do not erase distinctions where clarity matters. We tear down the walls of pride. We confront the impulse to protect our group more than we protect the Gospel. We name the temptation to elevate tradition above Scripture. We confess when our confessional loyalty overshadows our cross-centered identity. There are times when walls must stand:

- Against false teachers
- Against distorted gospels
- Against wolves dressed as shepherds

But many of our current walls are not protecting truth—they're preserving tribe. And it's time we tear those down.

Use the Confession. Preach the Gospel. Make the Difference Clear.

Use the confession. Absolutely. Let it guide your teaching. Let it help disciple the flock. Let it safeguard doctrinal purity in your church. But do not confuse it with the Gospel.

- The Gospel is the life, death, resurrection, and return of Jesus.

- The Gospel is the power of God unto salvation (Romans 1:16).
- The Gospel is the message we will still be celebrating in eternity.

Your confession is not your message. It helps define the message. It does not replace it. When believers are more fluent in their theological systems than in the Scriptures, when churches quote confessions more than they quote Christ, when unity is contingent upon secondary agreement rather than primary redemption—we've crossed a line the early Church never would have dared to draw.

The Reformation Reclaimed the Gospel. Let's Not Bury It Again.

The Reformers wrote confessions not to divide the Church into cliques, but to reclaim the Gospel from corruption. They were not trying to create a new class of believers—they were trying to call the Church back to Christ. Their goal was not to build theological skyscrapers. Their goal was to lay Gospel foundations again—where the Church had drifted into shadows.

We honor their courage not by entrenching ourselves in their language, but by embodying their posture: Christ alone, grace alone, faith alone, Scripture alone, to the glory of God alone. Let us not use the confessions they wrote to rebuild the walls they tore down.

Gospel Bridges Are Carried, Not Constructed

You don't get to build the bridge between two camps. You carry the cross—and lay it down across the divide. That is what Christ did. He became the bridge. He bore the cost.

A HOUSE DIVIDED

He spanned the gap between Jew and Gentile, heaven and earth, holiness and sin.

If we are going to walk in His footsteps, we must learn to carry that same cross between our camps. To lay down our need to be superior. To lay down our insistence on sameness. And to walk toward one another—carrying grace and gravity together.

Watchman's Commission

You, Watchman, are not called to be a brand ambassador. You are not called to be a system defender above all. You are called to see the wall and name it. To see the bridge and walk it.

Do not be ashamed of your confession. But let your boast be in the Gospel. Let your walls protect the sheep. Let your love reach across the gaps. Because at the end of the age, when the Bride is presented to the Lamb, there will not be sections for Calvinist, Charismatic, Anglican, or Free Church.

There will be only one Bride.
One Lamb.
One Gospel.
One eternal Kingdom.

Watchman's Prayer

Lord, Tear down every wall we've built in Your name—but without Your heart. Let truth remain, but let love flow. Teach us to hold the line on the essentials—and to hold one another with grace. Make us one—not in method, but in mission. Not in uniformity, but in unity.

In Jesus's name,
Amen.

9

Recovering Servant Leadership

Reclaiming Humility & Accountability in Spiritual Authority

The Basin and the Spotlight

There are two symbols of leadership in the modern Church. One is ancient and nearly forgotten: a basin of water and a towel. The other is modern and ever-present: a spotlight. The basin speaks of humility and the willingness to kneel. The spotlight speaks of charisma and the hunger to be seen. Though both claim to serve the Church, only one resembles Christ.

The basin waits in the corner, heavy with silence. It is not glamorous. It does not trend. But it is the tool Jesus picked up when He wanted to show us what greatness looked like.

The spotlight demands attention. It centers the stage. It brightens the gifted and raises the likable. Even truth can be repackaged as performance. And while it may illuminate, it often blinds. Jesus chose the basin. We often choose the spotlight. He stooped. We brand. He poured water. We pour content. He knelt. We climb. The Kingdom of God does not advance on curated platforms. It advances through sacrifice and the quiet obedience of those willing to serve in secret.

The early Church had no stage, yet it turned the world upside down (Acts 17:6). Why? Because it was led by people who had seen the risen Christ and knew the highest place in His Kingdom was still at His feet.

The Church has not lacked leaders. But we have often lacked servants who lead. We've built ministries on gifting, not godliness—mistaking influence for integrity. And people aren't walking away from the Gospel because they've studied it carefully.

They're walking away because they've watched us. Too often, what they see are voices that command, but rarely confess. Platforms that promote, but do not protect.

Jesus chose the basin—not because He lacked authority, but because He understood it. True greatness washes feet. True power gives, not grasps. And in His Kingdom, the towel is not optional. It is the test of whether we truly follow the King.

Spiritual Authority Begins at the Feet, Not the Head

The greatest rebuke to modern leadership is not found in a sermon or scandal. It is found in a towel.

> *"Jesus... rose from supper. He laid aside his outer garments, and taking a towel, tied it around his waist. Then he poured water into a basin and began to wash the disciples' feet..."—John 13:4-5*

This was not an illustration. It was not theater. It was the King of Glory—on His knees—washing the dirt from the feet of men who would soon desert Him. He did not demand service. He gave it. He did not take honor. He laid it down. In that moment, He redefined authority for every generation. In the Kingdom, authority descends. The world climbs. Jesus knelt. The world demands titles. Jesus took a towel. His throne was not built by applause, but by suffering. His crown was not won through charisma, but by crucifixion. When He rose from the table, He wasn't abandoning authority—He was revealing it.

> *"If I then, your Lord and Teacher, have washed your feet, you also ought to wash one another's feet."—John 13:14*

This was not suggestion. It was a standard. He didn't say:

> *"You ought to teach like Me."*

He said:

> *"You ought to wash like Me."*

Because until a leader is willing to kneel, they have no business standing over anyone.

The Cost of Celebrity Shepherds

We are witnessing a crisis of leadership—not for lack of talent, but for lack of trust. The headlines no longer surprise us. Scandal. Resignation. Collapse. Not from enemies of the Gospel—but from its most visible defenders. These leaders filled stadiums, launched podcasts, and pioneered movements. But they fell. And with them, trust fell. Charisma cannot carry character. And gifting, unguarded, becomes dangerous. The tragedy is not just their fall. It's that we elevated them in ways Jesus never did. We built platforms, not roots. We celebrated talent, not fruit. We confused visibility with maturity—and paid the price.

Jesus warned us:

> *"The hired hand... sees the wolf coming and leaves the sheep and flees... because he cares nothing for the sheep."—John 10:12–13*

Hired hands are impressive. They inspire crowds. But when danger comes, they disappear—because their platform was never built to protect.

The hired hand is not just indifferent—he is dangerous. He does not fight for the sheep because he never saw them as his responsibility. He values safety over sacrifice, optics over obedience. And when the wolf appears, his absence speaks louder than his sermons.

Jesus doesn't entrust His flock to those who perform well. He entrusts it to those who bleed when the sheep are attacked. And the sheep suffer. We've traded 1 Timothy 3's qualifications for Instagram optics. A man can preach with fire and be filled with pride. A woman can lead crowds and lack holiness. A platform can grow while private obedience collapses. Charisma is not fruit. It's not a gift of the Spirit. And when it's not crucified, it becomes a hazard.

Paul warned that leaders must be tested and not recent converts. Because without deep roots, collapse is only a matter of time. And the damage isn't just institutional—it's generational. Ask the young pastor who now fears trusting anyone. Ask the faithful elder whose flock scattered. Ask the unbeliever who mocks the Gospel because its messengers fell.

Jesus never asked us to be famous. He asked us to be faithful. But fame isolates. It insulates. And when gifting is excused from accountability, wolves enter. When a platform collapses, it's not just the leader who falls. It's the marriages they counseled. The young believers they shaped. The staff who trusted them. The children baptized by their hand. And yet—we keep building taller stages.

We keep handing out influence without testing character. We keep choosing speakers over shepherds. If you are a leader—pause. Would you still lead if the spotlight disappeared? Jesus entrusted His Church not to the most eloquent, but to the most broken. Peter—who wept over failure. Paul—who once persecuted the Body.

We don't need more platforms. We need more repentance. Because the Church is not built on charisma. It is built on faithfulness.

Jesus, the Foot-Washing King

John 13 is not sentimental. It's a spiritual earthquake—quiet, low, history-shifting. The Son of God did not sit on a throne. He knelt on a floor. He didn't issue decrees. He scraped dirt from between toes. This is not a parable.

It is the Gospel on display: the Highest stooping to serve the unworthy. Jesus knew the hour had come. He knew the cross was near. He knew betrayal was sitting at the table. And still—He rose. Not to correct. Not to escape. But to serve.

> *"Jesus... rose from supper. He laid aside His outer garments, and taking a towel, tied it around His waist... and began to wash the disciples' feet..."*
> —John 13:4–5

The hands that shaped galaxies now wiped mud. The fingers that healed blindness now cleaned callouses. And the disciples didn't understand. He washed Peter's feet—

knowing the denial. He washed Thomas' feet—knowing the doubt. He washed Judas' feet—knowing the betrayal. No foot was too dirty. No disciple too disappointing. His love did not flinch. His humility did not recoil. His authority did not excuse Him from service. It compelled Him to it.

> *"If I then, your Lord and Teacher, have washed your feet, you also ought to wash one another's feet."—John 13:14*

Jesus didn't just tell us to serve—He showed us. The world says climb. Jesus says descend. The world says brand. Jesus says break. The world says lead from strength. Jesus led in surrender.

> *"Whoever wants to be great among you must be your servant... even as the Son of Man came not to be served but to serve."—Matthew 20:26–28*

This is not a seasonal posture. It's a permanent one. The towel was not a prelude to the cross. It was glory in motion.

Jesus didn't graduate from the basin—He carried it all the way to Calvary. He served until it killed Him. He submitted until it crushed Him. He loved until He was forsaken. And that is why He is worthy. Because the King knelt—before He was crowned.

Authority That Protects, Not Projects

Authority, in the Kingdom of God, is not ornamental. It is not aesthetic. It is not performative. It is protective. It does not exist to elevate the leader—it exists to preserve the body. It does not serve the one who holds it—it serves those under its care. And when authority becomes projection rather than protection, it ceases to reflect Christ and begins to resemble the very systems He came to dismantle.

We live in a generation saturated with projection. Influence has replaced intimacy. Content has replaced character. And many in leadership now measure spiritual impact by reach, not responsibility. But biblical authority has never been about reach. It has always been about responsibility.

A Shepherd's Staff Is for Guarding, Not Branding

Authority in the Kingdom of God is not for display. It's not ornamental. It's not performative. It is protective. It doesn't elevate the leader. It preserves the body. It doesn't promote a brand. It carries a burden.

A shepherd's staff is not a stage prop. It's a guide and a guard. He feeds. He warns. He binds wounds. He weeps. He sacrifices.

That's what authority is meant to do:

- Feed the sheep with truth
- Protect from wolves
- Correct in love
- Walk through valleys

Paul understood this:

> *"Serving the Lord with all humility and with tears and with trials..."—Acts 20:19*

His ministry wasn't polished. It was costly. He didn't guard a reputation. He guarded people. Authority that bullies isn't biblical. Authority that manipulates isn't anointed. Peter warned plainly:

> *"Shepherd... not domineering... but being examples to the flock."—1 Peter 5:2–3*

Authority that creates fear is not Christlike. It may hold the crown—but it has lost the Spirit. True leaders don't perform from stages. They bleed in silence. They grieve when others stray. They pray more than they post. They take the first wounds when wolves attack. And they stay close. Because a shepherd cannot guard sheep from a distance.

Projected authority promotes persona. But spiritual authority requires presence. Jesus touched the sick. He wept at tombs. He paused for outcasts. He stayed close.

Let authority kneel again. Let it serve again. Let it stay when others leave. Let it protect when others exploit. Christ didn't entrust His Church to influencers. He gave it to shepherds. And shepherds don't project—they protect.

If You Cannot Be Corrected, You Should Not Lead

Correction is not a threat to leadership—it is its proving ground. A man who cannot be rebuked cannot be trusted. A woman who resists accountability is already unqualified. Because in the Kingdom, authority begins with submission, not status.

Too many believe gifting exempts them from correction. But even Jesus submitted—to the Father, in all things (John 5:19; Philippians 2:8). If the Son of God did not lead apart from submission, who are we to think we should?

Many leaders today isolate themselves—surrounded by yes-men, insulated by admiration, unreachable by truth. This is not spiritual leadership. It is tyranny.

> *"The way of a fool is right in his own eyes, but a wise man listens to advice."—Proverbs 12:15*

Leaders who cannot be corrected:

- Confuse respect with reverence'
- Mistake silence for agreement
- Create fear instead of trust

And over time, they stop serving the Body. They serve the image they've built. But the Word says:

> *"The Lord disciplines the one He loves…"*
> *—Hebrews 12:6*

A godly leader welcomes correction. They know the danger of drifting. They fear unchecked pride. David, though a king, confessed:

> *"I have sinned against the Lord."*
> *—2 Samuel 12:13*

He didn't hide behind position. He fell before truth. Leadership scandals share this trait: the leader could not be confronted. Paul rebuked Peter—publicly—when compromise crept in (Galatians 2:11). These were not power plays. They were men being shaped by God—through one another. No one in the New Testament led without correction. And no one should now. We need leaders who:

- Confess before collapse
- Invite rebuke before exposure
- Fear sin more than critique
- Surround themselves with truth-speakers, not fans

A HOUSE DIVIDED

The test of leadership is not how well you speak—
But how humbly you listen when truth knocks.

Submission to Christ Demands Humility in His Name

To lead in Christ's name is to submit in Christ's manner. Anything less is contradiction. Anything more is theft. Humility is not optional in the Kingdom. It's the very nature of the King. Christ doesn't entrust leadership to those who admire Him publicly but resist Him privately. He entrusts it to those who submit, tremble, and follow.

We forget this in an age of platforms. We confuse visibility with validity. We confuse charisma with character. But the New Testament treats leadership as a crucible—not a brand.

> *"Have this mind among yourselves, which is yours in Christ Jesus, who... emptied Himself... humbled Himself... became obedient to death..."*
> —*Philippians 2:5–8*

This is not decoration. It's blueprint. If Christ descended, what excuse have we to ascend? The Gospels have no space for personal empire. The epistles have no tolerance for ego-driven elders. Acts never celebrates status. Revelation doesn't share the throne. Every biblical model of leadership bears the marks of:

- Humility
- Dependency
- Repentance
- Sacrificial love

And every counterfeit bears the marks of:

- Control

- Pride
- Isolation
- Image

What we tolerate in leadership becomes what we reproduce in discipleship. If our leaders aren't submitted, our people won't surrender. Authority is real—and when it's godly, it's:

1. Accountable – no one leads alone.
2. Measured – never self-appointed or domineering
3. Rooted in truth – not in charisma or trend
4. Fruit-bearing – marked by the Spirit, not spectacle.

True leadership always looks like Christ. And Christ knelt.

"He humbled Himself..."—Philippians 2:8

So must we.

Pick Up the Towel Again

The crisis in the Church is not a lack of gifting. It is a lack of washing. We know how to preach, platform, and plan. We know how to capture attention. But do we know how to kneel? Somewhere along the way, the towel became metaphor. We became hearers of the Word—preaching the towel, framing it in sermons—but not doers (James 1:22–25). And like a man who forgets his reflection, we forget what leadership looks like in the mirror of Christ.

The towel is not a concept. It is a command. We framed it. We taught from it. But we stopped using it.

And the result?

A Church filled with admired leaders—who no

longer carry the basin. Jesus hasn't changed. His call hasn't softened:

> *"If I, your Lord and Teacher, have washed your feet, you also ought to wash one another's feet."*
> —John 13:14

This isn't sentiment. It's command. And the Church will not heal until we take it seriously again. The world doesn't need spiritual entrepreneurs. It needs foot-washers. Not more conferences. More consecration. Not strategists. Shepherds.

The leaders the world needs:

- Mourn in secret for the sins of the Body
- Fast more than they brand
- Stay behind to comfort
- Weep long after the livestream ends

These are the leaders heaven knows by name.

If You Lead: Wash Feet

No one is too gifted to kneel. If God gave you people—He also gave you a towel. Use it. Wash the feet of the slow, the wandering, the disillusioned. Wash anyway. Because that's what Jesus did. And if you feel invisible—remember: the towel touches eternity, not Instagram.

If You Follow: Pray for Those Who Lead

The towel is heavy. It absorbs more pain than praise. So pray. Intercede. Encourage. Don't idolize leaders—but don't abandon them either. Challenge their drift. Honor their obedience. Because no leader stands without warfare. And no leader lasts without prayer.

Hold Them Accountable—But Not Alone When leaders fall, we often ask, "How could they?" Better to ask, "Who told them they couldn't?" Accountability is not cruelty. It's care. That care must be structured. Leaders need guardrails—not just goodwill.

Establish elder plurality. Create spaces where confession is welcomed, not weaponized. Normalize shared leadership over celebrity personas. Ensure every leader is reachable, correctable, and surrounded by truth-tellers—not just fans.

Accountability is not a suspicion of leadership. It is the soil in which godly leadership thrives. Honor leaders enough to confront in love—before collapse becomes the teacher. Because the Kingdom is not built by the famous. It is built by the faithful.

> *"Well done, good and faithful servant."*
> *—Matthew 25:21*

The spotlight fades. The towel lasts.

Watchman's Prayer:

Lord, Raise up shepherds who fear no one but You. Leaders who serve before they speak. Who love before they lead. Who kneel before they climb. Strip us of titles that lack tears. Dismantle every platform not built on prayer. Tear down every throne where pride still rules. And return us to the upper room, where you washed the feet of failures, and called them friends. Restore the towel to the pulpit. Restore the basin to the boardroom. Restore the basin to the heart of the leader who still believes You came not to be served—but to serve.

In Jesus' name,
Amen.

10

A Watchman's Call To The Remnant

A Burden-Bearer's Duty to Defend Truth in An Age of Compromise

The Cracked Wall Still Stands

The wall is cracked—but it has not collapsed. You can still see the outline of what once was: A structure built not by men alone, but with prayer, blood, and Scripture etched into stone. It once stood tall—sheltering the weary, defending the sacred, declaring: "Here dwells the truth."

Now, it leans. Its joints are weakened. The mortar has thinned where compromise crept in. The stones groan beneath neglect. The gates creak on rusted hinges, and wind whistles through the breaches like old hymns—once sung in fire, now faint in the fog.

The wall has seen better days. It has weathered storms, betrayals, movements, and apathy. It stood when crowds gathered—and when they left. It has been repainted, rebranded, rebuilt in haste. Yet it still stands. Not because of present strength. Not because of structure or strategy. But because a remnant remains.

The Remnant Has Always Been the Reason

The wall should have fallen. But it hasn't—because in every generation, God preserves a people. Not a majority. Not a movement. A remnant. They don't trend. They don't perform. They don't bow to Baal or dilute the Gospel. They're not platformed, but they are preserved. They see what others excuse, tremble at the Word, and feel what others silence.

They are Watchmen. Not popular prophets—but burden-bearers. They don't argue for attention. They listen—between the silence of sermons and the fog of production. And what they hear burdens them. They see cracks—and won't call it creativity. They hear compromise—and won't applaud it. They watch the Church drift—and refuse to go along quietly. The world calls them rigid. The Church often calls them divisive. But Heaven calls them necessary.

The Watchman Does Not Argue to Win—He Speaks to Warn

You don't need a pulpit to be a Watchman. You don't need a platform, a title, or an audience. All you need is this: A Word from the Lord—and a heart that burns too deeply to stay silent. Watchmen are not appointed by men. They are assigned by God. Not all are Watchmen—but all are called to watch.

Every believer is called to vigilance: "Be sober-minded; be watchful..." (1 Peter 5:8).

The Watchman may carry a unique burden—but the Church carries a shared responsibility. To guard truth. To resist drift. To pray, discern, and stand. Some blow the trumpet. All must hear it. They don't critique to be clever. They speak because they must.

> *"Son of man, I have made you a watchman... hear the word I speak and give them warning from me."*
> —*Ezekiel 33:7*

This is not commentary. It is commission. And to ignore it is not preference—it is disobedience.

Not Critics, But Custodians

Today, spiritual analysis has become entertainment. But a Watchman isn't a content creator dissecting sermons for views. He doesn't throw stones to prove he's right. He warns with tears—because he knows judgment is near. He trembles before he speaks. He prays before he posts. He weeps before he warns. His motive is not applause. It is obedience.

He Speaks Because He Sees

He sees what others dismiss:

- Doctrine drifting
- Leadership compromising
- Wolves disguised in branded obedience

He speaks not to shame—but to awaken. Not for results—but because he's been entrusted with truth. Like Jeremiah, he may shout into silence. Like Noah, he may warn without applause. Like Stephen, his final word may be met with stones. Still, he speaks.

He Fights Forgetfulness, Not Flesh

The Church isn't dying from lack of content—but from lack of clarity. We've traded the sword of the Spirit for the tone of talk shows. But the Watchman remembers. He does not edit truth to preserve image. He does not soften the message to grow crowds. He is accountable—not to consensus—but to the King. To speak truth is to bleed for it. He knows the cost. He knows the rejection. But the fire of the Word will not let him stay silent. He is not here to win. He is here to be faithful.

Truth-Tellers in an Age of Compromise

The world rarely rewards truth-tellers. It does not applaud prophets. It does not celebrate the voices who cut through spiritual fog with holy fire. But Heaven remembers.

Elijah stood alone. Jeremiah wept alone. John the Baptist thundered—and died in prison. Polycarp was burned. Bonhoeffer was hanged. Millions more—unknown to history but precious in glory—stood, spoke, and suffered. They were not famous. They were faithful.

They Feared God More Than Backlash

These were not cultural influencers. They were Christ-followers. They didn't study algorithms. They studied Scripture. They didn't reshape the message to attract allies. They let the message reshape them—until obedience cost everything. And even when the world called them irrelevant, they didn't bend. Because they feared God's silence more than man's praise.

Standing Alone Is Not Standing in Vain

Truth is never truly alone. When Elijah fled, God reminded him:

> *"I have preserved 7,000 who have not bowed..."*
> *—1 Kings 19:18*

There is always a remnant. And God sees them.

- The pastor who refuses to dilute the Gospel
- The believer who stands when silence would be safer
- The disciple who chooses Scripture over strategy

They are known—not by platforms, but by purity.

When Unity Replaces Truth

Modern churches celebrate "unity"—until truth offends. We call it "loving" to let wolves roam free. We call it "peace" to silence warnings. We praise "gentleness" while doctrine is hollowed out. This is not the way of the cross. It is compromise disguised as compassion.

The Watchman Has Already Been Reshaped

He has been broken by the burden. He has wept through compromise. And so, when the Church tolerates what God condemns, the Watchman cries out—not in hatred, but in holy grief. He will be misunderstood. But he must not be muzzled. He speaks because silence would be betrayal. Because the truth still matters. Because faithfulness still matters.

John's Letters to Sardis Still Speak

A HOUSE DIVIDED

Revelation 3 opens with a piercing diagnosis:

> *"You have a reputation for being alive, but you are dead. Wake up. Strengthen what remains..."*
> —*Revelation 3:1–2*

Sardis wasn't persecuted. It wasn't heretical. It wasn't immoral. It was asleep. It faced no persecution—because it posed no threat to darkness. Sardis had no wolves at the gate, no rage from Rome, no fires of trial. And that may be the greatest tragedy of all. The enemy doesn't waste his weapons on a church that slumbers.

A church with momentum—but no movement of the Spirit. Programs—but no power. Reputation—but no repentance.

Image Over Integrity

Sardis had mastered the optics. The services stirred emotions. The leaders inspired crowds. But Heaven saw no life. They had built a name—and forgotten their need. They traded urgency for image. Obedience for production. Truth for trends.

Today's Sardis Streams in HD

We see Sardis in churches that attract the masses but avoid repentance. In preachers who go viral but rarely go deep. In pulpits optimized for influence—but void of consecration. The tragedy wasn't irreligion. It was appearance without substance. A glow without a flame.

The Warning Still Stands

Jesus didn't say start over. He said: "Wake up. Strengthen what remains."

There is something left to recover:

- The Word—still living
- The Spirit—still present
- The remnant—still watching

But revival won't come by repackaging. It will come by returning.

The Remnant Remains

Even in Sardis, Jesus says:

> *"Yet you have still a few names in Sardis, people who have not soiled their garments, and they will walk with me in white, for they are worthy."*
> —*Revelation 3:4*

They may sit in the back, praying quietly, grieving what's been lost. But Heaven sees them. And the promise is theirs.

Watchman: Strengthen What Remains

You are not called to rebuild the institution. You are called to rekindle the flame.

- Preach the Word again.
- Weep again.
- Kneel again.
- Refuse reputation.
- Embrace reality.

Jesus' letter still speaks. And so must we.

A HOUSE DIVIDED

Burden Without Bitterness

The Watchman carries a weight most never see. He weeps over compromise. He sees what others ignore. He speaks when others soften. But if he's not careful, his burden can turn to bitterness.

Discernment Without Love Becomes Suspicion

Many truth-tellers are shaped by deep disappointment. They've watched leaders fall. They've wept through hollow services. But pain, left unprayed, hardens. Discernment becomes suspicion. Boldness becomes bludgeoning. Truth becomes tyranny.

The Watchman Is Not a Watchdog

There is a difference between guarding truth and guarding pride. Watchdogs bark. Watchmen cry. Watchdogs posture. Watchmen intercede. One seeks to control. The other to deliver. The Watchman warns from love—not from disdain.

Bitterness Is a Broken Mirror

Bitterness is not strength—it's a wound disguised as clarity. It whispers, "They should've listened." It shouts, "I'm the only one left." But God does not anoint contempt. He anoints compassion. Even true words lose power when spoken from a bitter heart.

Truth Must Be Carried with Worship

Jeremiah wept because he still loved. His warnings were

soaked in reverence. Truth without reverence becomes performance. But truth with worship cuts clean—not cruel. Jesus is our model. He warned—and He wept. He rebuked—but from love, not pride.

The Watchman's Test

Can you carry the fire without being consumed by it?

- Can you hold the line without coldness?
- Can you grieve for the ones who reject you?
- Can you speak with conviction and still carry tears?

Because when the tears stop, so does heaven's weight.

The Servant, Not the Sheriff

You are not the Church's sheriff. You are the King's servant. Speak with His grief. Warn with His urgency. Serve with His tenderness. Let your voice remain sharp— But keep your soul soft.

Sound the Warning. Bear the Weight. Preach Without Twisting

There are moments when silence is betrayal. This is one of them.

Truth Is Not Negotiable

Truth is not trendy. It is not a suggestion. It is not flexible in tone or fragile in content. Truth is a Person—Jesus Christ—full of grace and truth (John 1:14). To follow Him means to hold what He held, say what He said, and resist what He rebuked. We cannot edit truth for comfort. We must not present a crown and hide the cross.

Preach Without Twisting

Many today preach a soft gospel:

- Love without repentance
- Grace without judgment
- Faith without endurance

It attracts crowds. It sells books. But it does not make disciples. You are not called to preach what works. You are called to preach what's true.

"Preach the Word; be ready in season and out..."
—*2 Timothy 4:2*

The Word is not ours to adjust. It is ours to announce.

The Weight Is Real

Preaching truth carries cost. You may lose invitations. You may be misunderstood. You may be maligned by the very ones you're trying to protect. But the burden proves the call. Ezekiel was warned:

"If you do not speak... their blood I will require at your hand."—*Ezekiel 33:6*

This is not hyperbole. It is holy responsibility.

Warning Is Worship

To warn is not harshness—it is reverence. It is obedience

to the Word that burns within. You do not warn because you want to win. You warn because you fear silence more than scorn.

The Church Needs Obedience, Not Just Opinions

We are not lacking voices. We are lacking conviction. We need preachers who tremble before they preach. Teachers who fear twisting more than trending. Watchmen who choose obedience over optics.

Speak When It's Easier to Be Silent

Silence may feel safe. But it is not faithfulness. "Winsomeness" that hides truth is just cowardice in soft tones. There is a time for kindness— But this is also a time for clarity. If we do not speak, we are not stewards.

Serve When It's Easier to Walk Away

Yes, the burden is heavy. But it was never meant to be easy. You were given fire—not for fame, but for faithfulness. You were called to endure—not to escape. Preach without twisting. Warn without wavering. Love without watering down. Even if you're the last one on the wall—stand anyway.

The Wall Can Be Rebuilt. The Watchman Must Not Be Silent

Return to the wall—the one from Chapter 1. Still fractured. Still groaning. Still cracked. But now—movement. A figure walks the perimeter. Not an engineer. Not a leader. A Watchman. Not the strongest—but the faithful. He doesn't carry blueprints. He carries burden. He kneels, lifts a stone, and places it—not to impress, but to obey. Another joins—

A HOUSE DIVIDED

intercession on her lips. Then a shepherd arrives—not to speak, but to labor. They don't form a committee. They don't publish a plan. They build—quietly, faithfully, stone by stone.

The Remnant Rebuilds

It won't be the influencers. It won't be the loud. This rebuilding is too sacred for spectacle. It's not forged in conferences—but in closets. Not broadcast with noise—but born in trembling. This is the work of Watchmen.

The Watchman Builds What Others Forgot

He's not a doom-shouter. He doesn't only name the cracks—he fills them. He preaches truth. He disciples with tears. He stands with resolve, even when it's mocked. And with each act of obedience, the wall lives again.

The Remnant Was Made for This

They aren't museum keepers. They aren't retreating into fear or nostalgia. They remember what was—but they live for what must be. Driven not by anger, but by assignment. They don't wait for perfect conditions. They move—because the King has not yet returned.

If the Watchman Is Silent, the City Sleeps

If he doesn't speak:

- Truth fades
- Doctrine drifts
- Holiness weakens

But if he speaks—Even alone—the wall is not lost. Hope lives in obedient voices. No applause required. No titles needed. Only faithfulness:

- To speak when it costs
- To kneel when it's lonely
- To carry the stone again and again

As long as the Watchman speaks, the wall can rise. And if the wall stands—So does the Church.

Final Charge: Strengthen What Remains

> *"Strengthen what remains and is about to die."*
> *—Revelation 3:2*

This is not a suggestion. It is a charge. These words echo through every compromised generation. They are not just for Sardis. They are for us—now.

The Hour Demands Action

The days ahead will not be gentle. False teachers won't silence themselves. Culture will not wait for the Church to catch up. This is not the time to retreat. It is the time to rebuild.

What remains?

- The unchanging truth of the Word
- The presence of the Spirit
- The holiness of God
- The power of the Gospel
- The voice of the Watchman

A HOUSE DIVIDED

They are still alive—but under siege.

Strengthen the Word

Do not soften it to suit the age. Do not bend it to gain favor. Let Scripture shape your message—Not trends, polls, or preferences. Proclaim the Word until it breaks you—And rebuilds those who hear it.

Strengthen the Altar

Worship is not performance. It is posture. God is not after soundtracks. He is after surrender. Call the Church back to the altar—Where songs are born in repentance, And fire falls on holy ground.

Strengthen the Pulpit

The pulpit is not for personalities. It is for prophets. Preach with clarity, not cleverness. Lift Christ—whether or not anyone claps. Fear God more than losing favor. Let conviction burn hotter than applause.

Strengthen the Watchmen

We need fewer critics and more intercessors. Voices who tremble before they speak. Watchmen who won't be dulled by mockery Or hardened by hatred. Let them remember: They were not called to trend—but to testify.

Strengthen What's Worth Fighting For

The Church is not a brand. She is the Bride. Wounded?

Yes. But not abandoned. And her Groom still calls for her to be made ready.

So:

- Strengthen her doctrine
- Strengthen her holiness
- Strengthen her love for truth
- Strengthen her courage to endure

This Is Your Charge Not to impress. Not to ascend in visibility. But to stay faithful.

- To bear the burden
- To lift the Word
- To kneel in prayer
- To speak with reverence

Not for applause—but because Heaven is watching. And When the King Returns... He will not ask about your reach.

> *"For we must all appear before the judgment seat of Christ..."—2 Corinthians 5:10*

Not to be measured by numbers. Not by applause. But by obedience.

> *"So then each of us will give an account of himself to God."—Romans 14:12*

That Day is not metaphor. It is appointed. And the question will not be:

> *"Were you followed?"*

but

"Were you faithful?"

He will ask:

- Were you faithful?
- Did you speak truth when it was costly?
- Did you strengthen what remained?

And if you did—He will say:

"Well done, good and faithful servant. You have strengthened what remained. Now enter into your reward."

A Watchman's Final Question

To the believer rooted in tradition, denomination, or movement—this is not a rebuke, but a reckoning. This book was not written to elevate one camp over another, but to remind every soul: The only hill worth dying on is the one where Christ already bled.

So ask yourself soberly: If you truly listen to the warnings in these pages—what do you lose?

Perhaps a theological label.

Perhaps a system you've trusted.

Perhaps the comfort of believing your group has it more right than the rest.

You may lose the applause of your circle. You may lose the ease of inherited beliefs. You may even lose the pride of thinking God only works through people who look like you, worship like you, or preach like you.

But you will not lose Christ.

If your convictions are grounded in truth, then testing them against Scripture will only deepen them. If your worship is pure, it will endure even under the fire of examination. If your doctrine exalts Christ and clings to His Word, it will not crumble when measured by the full counsel of God. You may lose your echo chamber. But you will gain a sword, sharpened by the whole Body. You may lose comfort. But you will gain clarity.

So again:

If you're right, and this book is wrong—what have you lost by testing? Only a little pride. A little certainty. A little insulation.

But now ask the harder question:

If you're wrong—what do you lose? If your tradition has elevated man's teaching above God's Word... If your movement has trusted signs more than Scripture... If your denomination has divided the Body through pride disguised as purity... If your theology has explained away obedience, holiness, or the fear of the Lord...

Then what you lose is not small.

You risk building on sand, not stone. You risk making disciples of a system, not of Christ. You risk ignoring His voice because it didn't sound like your tribe. You risk being sincere—and sincerely deceived.

This isn't about being Charismatic or Cessationist, Reformed or Catholic, Baptist or Pentecostal, Anglican or Emergent, Independent or Institutional.

This is about whether Christ Himself is the cornerstone—or just a logo your camp builds around.

"If I am wrong, I lose only my pride.
But if you are wrong—you may be following a tradition
that exalts itself above the Truth."

The Watchman does not speak to score theological points. He speaks to warn the city.

So I ask you:

Test your beliefs. Test your leaders. Test your

fire. Test your fruit. Not by how familiar it feels—but by how faithful it is to what God has already spoken.

The Spirit and the Word will never contradict. And unity will never come by defending our camps—only by surrendering to the King.

Appendix

A Framework for Discernment in the Last Days

> *"for the weapons of our warfare are not of the flesh, but divinely powerful for the tearing down of strong holds..."*
> —*2 Corinthians 10:4*

In a time where Scripture is often filtered through denomination, tradition, or emotion, we need more than just sincerity—we need integrity. Not intellectualism. Not speculation. But biblical soundness rooted in reverence for what is written.

These five tests are not a system—they are a filter. They do not replace Scripture—they realign us to it. Use them to examine teachings, test doctrines, and guard your heart against confusion, cleverness, and compromise.

Language Consistency

Question: Does this interpretation match the original meaning of the Hebrew or Greek?

The Bible wasn't written in English. Many doctrinal

errors begin when we impose modern definitions onto ancient words. Language shapes theology—and misreading words can lead to misrepresenting God. "Agape" love is not emotional affection—it's sacrificial. "Confound their language" (Genesis 11:7) shows that division begins with distortion.

Discernment Tip: Use a trusted lexicon to understand key words in context. Guard against emotional interpretations that flatten biblical nuance.

Immediate Context Integrity

Question: Am I interpreting this verse in light of its surrounding chapter?

A verse without its context becomes a pretext. Many false teachings isolate one passage and ignore the full thought of the writer.

Example: 1 Corinthians 14:1–5 is often used to justify public tongues. But verses 27–28 clearly state: "If there is no interpreter, keep silent in the church."

Discernment Tip: Read the whole chapter.

Ask, "What point is the Holy Spirit making—not just what point can I make?"

Historical-Cultural Context

Question: What did this mean to the original audience?

Jesus and Paul spoke into specific cultures, under Roman law, within Jewish traditions. Understanding that context protects us from modern distortion. Hillel taught, "Do not do to others..." Jesus raised the standard: "Do unto others..." (Matthew 7:12). Context changes tone, urgency, and purpose.

Discernment Tip: Study the customs, religious expectations, and socio-political dynamics of the time. Let the Bible speak in its own world before applying it to yours.

But do not stop there. Application is not merely an intellectual exercise—it is a matter of wisdom. And wisdom is not achieved by study alone. It is given by the Holy Spirit, not conjured by the flesh (James 1:5; 1 Corinthians 2:12-14). The same Spirit who inspired the Word must illuminate its meaning and guide its faithful application (John 16:13). Without Him, even the most historically accurate interpretation can become misapplied.

So remember:

> *"The natural person does not accept the things of the Spirit of God... they are spiritually discerned."*
> *—1 Corinthians 2:14*

True discernment is birthed from a heart yielded to the Spirit and a mind anchored in the Word.

Theological Consistency

Question: Does this teaching contradict anythingelse Scripture clearly teaches?

Truth does not cancel itself out. Everydoctrine must agree with the whole counsel of God. The veil was torn at Christ's death(Matthew

27:51)—but access to the Father comes through the resurrected Jesus, not merely His crucifixion.

Discernment Tip: If a teaching introduces tension with core truths (the nature of God, salvation by grace, the mediating role of Christ), test it harder.

Christocentric Alignment

Question: Does this point to Jesus—or to man?

Jesus is the beginning, the middle, and the end of our faith. He is not just the doorway to truth—He is the truth. If a doctrine starts with Jesus but ends with man, it has missed the mark. The veil was torn through Jesus' flesh (Hebrews 10:20), and access to God is only through Him. Any teaching that finishes without Jesus as High Priest, King, and Judge has unfinished theology. Discernment Tip: Christ must be the lens through which we interpret everything. If He is not central, the teaching is off-center.

Final Word

Let the Bible Interpret the Bible. The Bible is not open to personal interpretation—it is open to faithful submission. Let these five tests serve not as gates, but as guardrails. They exist to keep the Church from drifting into deception and from building on doctrinal sand.

> *"Test everything; hold fast what is good."*
> *—1 Thessalonians 5:21*

Let God's Word interpret itself. Let Jesus remain the center. And let the Spirit guide—not our feelings, but our obedience.

Endnotes

This appendix contains the complete set of endnotes used throughout A House Divided: Rediscovering Unity in the Last Days. Each entry corresponds to a citation, historical allusion, scriptural reference, or theological source referenced within the chapters. Endnotes follow the order in which they appear and are grouped by chapter for clarity and consistency.

- All Scripture quotations, unless otherwise indicated, are taken from the King James Version (KJV) of the Bible.
- Historical and denominational facts are drawn from publicly available sources such as church history surveys, the Center for the Study of Global Christianity at Gordon-Conwell Theological Seminary, and primary historical records.
- Interpretations, summaries, and theological frameworks are aligned with the Watchman's conviction of the clarity, authority, and sufficiency of Scripture, without dependence on any denominational system.
- Historical references are used to illustrate patterns and spiritual principles, not to

elevate tradition above the revealed Word of God.
- The final typesetting of these notes should conform to the editorial standards selected during publication—such as Chicago Manual of Style, Turabian, or author-date format—while maintaining readability for a theologically engaged audience.

General Citation Standards

- Scripture Quotations
Default translation: English Standard Version (ESV), unless otherwise indicated.
Format: John 17:21, ESV
If paraphrased, the citation will reflect the theological intent without quotation marks.

- Books and Print Publications
J.I. Packer, Knowing God (Downers Grove, IL: IVP, 1973), 84.

- Web Sources
accessed April 20, 2025, https://...

- Creeds and Historical Documents
"The Nicene Creed," Council of Nicaea, AD 325.

Example Endnotes by Chapter

Chapter 1: The Fault Line Beneath the Church

1. Constantine's Edict of Milan in 313 AD legalized Christianity, marking a dramatic shift from persecution to institutional influence within Roman society.
2. The First Council of Nicaea (325 AD)and subsequent ecumenical councils established necessary boundaries for orthodoxy but also laid foundations for later structural divisions.
3. The Great Schism of 1054 formally divided the Church into Eastern Orthodox and Roman Catholic traditions, primarily over authority (papal primacy) and the filioque clause.
4. The Protestant Reformation (1517onward), initiated by Martin Luther, recovered essential doctrines like sola fide and sola scriptura, yet it also inadvertently modeled separation over reconciliation.
5. There are currently estimated to be over 40,000 Protestant denominations globally. This figure is cited by the Center for the Study of Global Christianity at Gordon-Conwell Theological Seminary.
6. Jeremiah 6:14 speaks of false prophets offering superficial peace, an apt warning for the modern Church's tendency to prefer the illusion of unity over true reconciliation.
7. John 17:17, 21 records Christ's high priestly prayer, anchoring unity in sanctification through truth, not sentimentality.
8. Matthew 12:25 (also referenced in Luke11:17) establishes the principle that internal division leads to collapse—a spiritual law with implications for both the Church and broader society.

9. Paul's plea for unity among the Corinthian believers (1 Corinthians 1:10-13) highlights the danger of aligning with personalities or camps rather than with Christ Himself.
10. Isaiah 28:16 and Psalm 118:22 prophetically describe Christ as the tested, precious cornerstone—fulfilled in the New Testament references such as 1 Peter 2:6-7 and 1 Corinthians 3:11.
11. Ephesians 4:3, 4-6 outlines the apostolic framework for unity: shared Spirit, shared Lord, shared baptism, shared Father—a theological foundation for true oneness in the Body.
12. Galatians 2 and Acts 15 recount examples where early Church leaders addressed doctrinal tension through correction and fellowship, not separation.
13. 1 Corinthians 3:11-13 warns that every builder's work will be tested by fire, reinforcing the accountability of all who contribute to the structure of Christ's Church.
14. The 1054 East-West Schism's unresolved theological tensions over issues like the filioque clause still reverberate today in separated Christian traditions.
15. John 13:35 emphasizes that the distinguishing mark of Christian discipleship is love for one another, which necessarily includes a commitment to visible unity.
16. Ephesians 4:16 portrays the Church as a living, interconnected body—not isolated institutions, but joined through mutual edification and truth.
17. Hebrews 12:27 references the divine shaking that removes what is unstable so that what is unshakable may remain, a prophetic warning to the Church today.
18. Nehemiah's rebuilding of Jerusalem's wall

(Nehemiah 2–6) serves as a biblical model for spiritual vigilance, persistence in opposition, and communal responsibility in restoring what has been broken.

Chapter 2: One Gospel, Many Options

1. 1 Corinthians 15:1–4 defines the Gospel as Christ's death, burial, and resurrection according to the Scriptures—the anchor of saving faith.
2. The practice of doctrinal triage—weighing primary, secondary, and tertiary doctrines—was notably emphasized by theologians like R. Albert Mohler Jr. but is grounded in the apostolic pattern seen in Acts 15, Romans 14, and 1 Corinthians 8.
3. Ephesians 4:14 warns against being "tossed to and fro by the waves and carried about by every wind of doctrine" without spiritual maturity.
4. Acts 15 records the Jerusalem Council, where the early Church clarified that Gentile believers were not bound to Mosaic law, affirming salvation by grace through faith alone.
5. Romans 14 and 1 Corinthians 8–10 address how believers should handle disputable matters, urging liberty with responsibility and unity without uniformity.
6. Galatians 2 recounts Paul confronting Peter when Peter's behavior endangered the clarity of the Gospel among Gentiles.
7. 2 Timothy 2:23 warns against "foolish and ignorant controversies" that produce quarrels rather than godliness.
8. 1 Timothy 1:3–7 describes teachers who devote

themselves to myths and endless genealogies, promoting speculation rather than the stewardship of faith.
9. Colossians 2:8 warns believers not to be taken captive by hollow philosophy and human tradition rather than Christ.
10. 1 John 4:1 commands believers to "test the spirits" because many false prophets have gone out into the world.
11. 1 Corinthians 1:10–13 rebukes factionalism among believers who rallied around personalities rather than the cross.
12. Ephesians 4:3–6 exhorts the Church to preserve unity by focusing on one Spirit, one Lord, one faith, one baptism, and one God.
13. Romans 14:1–12 shows Paul's pastoral heart for welcoming believers who differ on secondary matters, urging conscience-based freedom within the Body.
14. 1 Corinthians 8:1–13 contrasts knowledge, which "puffs up,"with love, which "builds up," warning against wounding weaker consciences.
15. John 16:13 promises that the Spirit of Truth will guide believers into all truth, but He does so progressively and faithfully, not instantaneously through every teacher.
16. 1 Corinthians 13:12 reminds us that "we see through a glass darkly," affirming the need for humility in non-essential doctrines.
17. 2 Timothy 4:3–4 warns that a time would come when people would not endure sound teaching but would accumulate teachers to suit their own passions.
18. 1 Corinthians 3:11 insists that no foundation can be

laid other than Jesus Christ, protecting the Church from shifting to secondary foundations.
19. 1 Corinthians 15:3-4 again highlights that the Gospel's death, burial, and resurrection are of "first importance"—the immovable center.
20. Romans 14:19 urges believers to "pursue what makes for peace and for mutual upbuilding," particularly when handling disputable matters.
21. Colossians 2:2-3 points to Christ as the One "in whom are hidden all the treasures of wisdom and knowledge," not concealed codes or private revelations.
22. Ephesians 4:11-16 calls for growth in truth and love, so that the Church may reach maturity and unity of faith, built on Christ as the Head.
23. Jude 1:3 commands believers to "contend for the faith that was once for all delivered to the saints," guarding the Gospel without creating new barriers.
24. Philippians 2:1-2 urges the Church to be "of the same mind, having the same love, being in full accord and of one mind" under the Lordship of Christ.
25. 2 Peter 1:20-21 reminds believers that no prophecy of Scripture comes from someone's own private interpretation but from the Spirit's inspiration.
26. Ephesians 2:19-22 describes the Church as a holy temple, built on the foundation of the apostles and prophets, Christ Jesus Himself being the cornerstone.
27. 1 Corinthians 4:6 admonishes believers "not to go beyond what is written," a rebuke against theological pride and unnecessary additions.
28. Revelation 2:4-5 warns the Church at Ephesus that doctrinal precision without love is not enough;

they must return to their first love—or have their lampstand removed.
29. Galatians 1:6–9 contains Paul's fierce warning against turning to "a different gospel"—even if it is proclaimed by an angel or apostle.
30. 2 Timothy 2:15 calls believers to rightly divide the Word of truth, distinguishing between essentials and non-essentials with wisdom and care.

Chapter 3: The Rise of Celebrity Christians

1. Exodus 32:1–6 records Israel's creation of the golden calf—not as open rebellion against worship, but as a reshaping of worship to fit their impatience and desires.
2. 2 Corinthians 11:4 warns the Church about receiving "another Jesus, another spirit, or another gospel" based on impressive packaging rather than truth.
3. Hebrews 13:17 reminds leaders that they will give an account for how they shepherd the flock—not for their popularity but for their faithfulness.
4. 1 Corinthians 1:13 confronts the early divisions in Corinth where loyalty to human leaders replaced allegiance to Christ.
5. 1 Corinthians 3:7 emphasizes that "neither he who plants nor he who waters is anything, but only God who gives the growth"—a correction against personality-driven ministry.
6. 1 Corinthians 2:3 highlights Paul's own posture before the Church: "I came to you in weakness and in fear and much trembling," rejecting celebrity-style ministry.
7. Matthew 23:5 critiques leaders who "do all their deeds to be seen by others," exposing the heart behind religious performance.

8. Luke 6:26 warns, "Woe to you when all people speak well of you," linking universal applause to the fate of false prophets.
9. 2 Corinthians 11:23–28 catalogues Paul's true resume of ministry: suffering, persecution, and burden for the churches—not acclaim.
10. 1 Timothy 5:22 counsels Timothy not to be hasty in laying hands on leaders, lest immature or untested individuals cause greater harm.
11. Titus 1:5–9 lays out the biblical qualifications for elders, focusing on character, sound doctrine, and self-control—not charisma or visibility.
12. 1 Corinthians 9:27 captures Paul's fear of being "disqualified" even after preaching to others, showcasing his deep humility.
13. James 3:1 issues a sober warning: "Not many of you should become teachers... for you know that we who teach will be judged with greater strictness."
14. Matthew 7:16 reminds that true leaders are known "by their fruits," not their following or fame.
15. Isaiah 66:2 declares that God esteems "the one who is humble and contrite in spirit, and trembles at My word"—not those who perform for applause.
16. John 10:12–13 contrasts the hireling, who flees when danger comes, with the true shepherd who lays down his life for the sheep.
17. Matthew 20:26–28 defines greatness in the Kingdom: not through lording over others, but by becoming a servant.
18. John 6:15 shows Jesus withdrawing when the crowds wanted to make Him king by force, refusing to be co-opted by popularity.
19. 2 Timothy 2:23 warns believers to avoid "foolish and ignorant controversies" that breed quarrels rather than godliness.

20. John 9:35 records God's voice declaring, "This is my beloved Son: hear Him," centering true authority and focus on Christ alone—not human leaders.
21. Romans 12:3 exhorts believers not to think of themselves more highly than they ought, but with sober judgment according to the measure of faith God has assigned.
22. Luke 9:46–48 records Jesus rebuking the disciples when they argued about who was the greatest, realigning ambition toward servanthood.
23. 1 Peter 5:2–3 instructs elders to "shepherd the flock of God that is among you, not domineering over those in your charge, but being examples to the flock."
24. John 15:16 reminds that Jesus chose His followers—not for platform-building, but for bearing lasting fruit.
25. Galatians 6:14 captures Paul's boast: "Far be it from me to boast except in the cross of our Lord Jesus Christ."
26. 2 Timothy 4:2–5 commands preachers to "preach the word; be ready in season and out of season; reprove, rebuke, and exhort, with complete patience and teaching," even when it is unpopular.
27. Revelation 3:17–19 rebukes the Laodicean Church for their self-sufficiency and calls them to renewed zeal and repentance.
28. 2 Corinthians 2:17 warns that "we are not like so many, peddlers of God's word, but as men of sincerity, as commissioned by God."
29. John 13:4–5 shows Jesus modeling servant leadership by washing the disciples' feet—choosing the towel over the throne.
30. Hebrews 12:28–29 reminds us that we are receiving a Kingdom that cannot be shaken, and so must

worship God with reverence and awe—not with spectacle.

Chapter 4: The Battles of Biblical Interpretation

1. Psalm 119:130 affirms the clarity of Scripture, declaring that the Word gives light and understanding even to the simple.
2. Jeremiah 23:29 portrays God's Word as a fire and a hammer, emphasizing its power to pierce and to transform.
3. 2 Timothy 3:16 teaches that all Scripture is inspired by God and is profitable for doctrine, reproof, correction, and instruction in righteousness.
4. Acts 17:11 describes the Bereans as noble because they examined the Scriptures daily to test the truth of what they heard—even from an apostle.
5. 1 Samuel 3:9 records the prayer of Samuel as he first learns to recognize the voice of God: "Speak, Lord, for your servant is listening."
6. John 1:14 affirms that the Word became flesh and dwelt among us—highlighting Jesus as the living revelation of God's truth.
7. Matthew 5:17 shows Jesus' affirmation that He came not to abolish the Law or the Prophets but to fulfill them.
8. Luke 24:27 recounts how Jesus, on the road to Emmaus, explained how all Scripture pointed to Himself, setting the standard for Christ-centered interpretation.
9. Matthew 4:4, 7, 10 reveals how Jesus countered Satan's twisted use of Scripture by rightly applying God's Word during His wilderness temptations.
10. Matthew 22:29 records Jesus' rebuke of the

Sadducees for not knowing the Scriptures or the power of God.
11. Luke 10:21 highlights that truth is revealed not to the wise in their own eyes, but to the humble like little children.
12. 1 Corinthians 1:12–13 rebukes the Corinthian Church for rallying around personalities rather than remaining united in Christ.
13. Galatians 2:20 defines the believer's true identity as crucified with Christ and alive only through Him—not by loyalty to theological tribes.
14. Romans 3:4 teaches that God must be true even if every man is a liar, anchoring final authority in God's Word.
15. 1 Corinthians 4:6 warns against going beyond what is written in Scripture—a principle of restraint and reverence in interpretation.
16. 1 Peter 4:11 calls those who speak to speak "as the oracles of God," stressing the responsibility of teaching with fidelity to divine truth.
17. Hebrews 4:12 depicts the Word of God as living, active, and sharper than any two-edged sword, cutting through heart and soul.
18. Psalm 46:10 commands believers to "be still" and know that He is God, reinforcing the need for silence and reverence before divine truth.
19. Luke 24:32 records the disciples' testimony that their hearts burned within them as Jesus opened the Scriptures to them.
20. John 10:27 emphasizes that Christ's sheep hear His voice—a call to spiritual intimacy through the Word, not merely intellectual assent.

Chapter 5: When Truth Is Torn

1. John 14:6 affirms that truth is not abstract, but personal—embodied fully in Jesus Christ Himself.
2. John 17:17, 21 presents Jesus' prayer for His followers, linking sanctification, truth, and unity directly as a testimony to the world.
3. John 8:32 declares that truth—not sentiment or flexibility—produces genuine freedom.
4. Matthew 12:25 warns that any house divided against itself cannot stand, underscoring division as fatal, not merely unfortunate.
5. John 12:32 points to Christ lifted up as the central "banner" that draws all men to Himself—not a brand, but a crucified Savior.
6. 1 Corinthians 1:12-13 records Paul's rebuke of factionalism in the Corinthian church, asking whether Christ Himself had been divided.
7. Ephesians 4:15 commands believers to "speak the truth in love," anchoring both boldness and relational humility in doctrinal maturity.
8. 1 Timothy 3:15 describes the Church as the "pillar and ground of the truth," highlighting that protecting truth is a core part of the Church's identity.
9. 1 Corinthians 13:2 reminds that even perfect theological knowledge, without love, amounts to nothing before God.
10. 2 Timothy 2:24 charges the Lord's servant not to be quarrelsome, but kind and patient in teaching—especially when correcting opponents.
11. Genesis 3:1 shows Satan's original strategy: to introduce doubt by questioning the clarity of God's Word.
12. 1 Corinthians 14:33 declares that God is not

the author of confusion, highlighting division and confusion as spiritual attacks, not neutral occurrences.
13. 2 Corinthians 2:11 exhorts believers not to be ignorant of Satan's schemes—particularly his divisive tactics.
14. John 17:21 emphasizes that the unity of the Church under truth serves a missional purpose: that the world may believe the Father sent the Son.
15. 1 Timothy 1:7 warns against those who desire to be teachers of the law but lack true understanding, cautioning against ego-driven leadership.
16. 1 Corinthians 9:27 reflects Paul's fear of being "disqualified," showing that even great leaders must guard humility and finish faithfully.
17. Isaiah 61:4 prophesies that God's people are called to rebuild ruins and repair devastations—a fitting image for the Church's current need to mend its breaches.
18. Matthew 12:25 (reiterated) underlines that division is a terminal condition unless addressed by repentance and truth.
19. Ephesians 4:3 calls believers to make every effort to maintain the unity of the Spirit in the bond of peace—not passive unity, but intentional guarding.
20. 1 Peter 4:11 exhorts those who speak to speak as the "oracles of God," reinforcing that interpretation, teaching, and correction must submit fully to divine authority, not tribal interpretation.

Chapter 6: Discerning Truth In A Noisy Church

1. 1 Kings 19:11–12 shows that God's voice is often not in the spectacle, but in the still, small voice.
2. Hebrews 5:14 ties spiritual maturity directly to

trained discernment, distinguishing good from evil.
3. 1 Thessalonians 5:21–22 commands believers to "test everything" and "hold fast" to what is good, affirming discernment as an act of faithfulness.
4. Acts 17:11 praises the Bereans for eagerly receiving the Word but also testing it against Scripture daily.
5. Galatians 1:6 highlights the danger of quickly deserting the true Gospel for distortions, emphasizing vigilance in doctrine.
6. Ephesians 4:14 warns against being tossed by every wind of doctrine, calling believers to grow into spiritual stability.
7. John 10:27 centers the call to discernment on intimacy with the Shepherd—"My sheep hear my voice."
8. Psalm 23:3 promises that God restores the soul and leads in righteousness, reminding the betrayed that healing is His work.
9. 1 John 2:19 explains that those who depart from true fellowship reveal that they were never truly part of it.
10. 1 Peter 4:11 exhorts those who speak to speak as the "oracles of God," reinforcing the call to faithful communication of truth.
11. John 17:17 anchors sanctification in truth, which is identified as God's Word.
12. Psalm 46:10 calls the believer to "be still" and know that He is God, a crucial discipline for discernment in a noisy world.
13. John 10:27 (reiterated) reaffirms that Christ's true sheep will recognize and follow His voice.
14. 2 Timothy 2:24–25 instructs the Lord's servant to correct opponents with gentleness, coupling discernment with humility.

15. Psalm 119:130 declares that the unfolding of God's words gives light and understanding to the simple.
16. John 10:27 (final reiteration) underscores that discernment flows from proximity to Christ, not from suspicion or striving.
17. Hebrews 4:12 describes the Word of God as a sharp sword, discerning thoughts and intentions, vital for authentic discernment.
18. John 17:21 shows that unity under truth is a witness to the world of Christ's divine sending.
19. 1 Corinthians 13:2 reminds that discernment or doctrinal knowledge without love amounts to nothing.
20. Revelation 2-3 reveals Christ's evaluation of churches, showing that discernment in the Church is a continuing call, not a past accomplishment.

Chapter 7: The Faces That Oppose Truth

1. Jude 1:3 calls believers to "earnestly contend for the faith which was once delivered unto the saints."
2. 1 Peter 3:15 commands us to give an answer for our hope "with meekness and fear," setting the posture of apologetics.
3. Matthew 13:1-23 (The Parable of the Sower) explains how the Word is received differently based on the condition of the heart.
4. 2 Timothy 2:25 teaches that correction must be given with meekness, as repentance is granted by God.
5. John 4 portrays the Samaritan woman, a wounded skeptic who encountered truth through tenderness and directness.
6. John 3 introduces Nicodemus, the intellectual who needed to move from knowledge to faith.

7. Acts 17 depicts Paul's engagement with the intellectual Athenians at Mars Hill.
8. Acts 8:1-3 shows Saul's angry persecution of the Church before his conversion.
9. Acts 8:9-24 presents Simon the Sorcerer, a charismatic deceiver seeking power without transformation.
10. Revelation 2:20 warns the Church against tolerating Jezebel, symbolizing spiritual manipulation and false prophecy.
11. Revelation 3:14-22 rebukes the Laodicean Church for its lukewarmness—spiritual apathy masked as faith.
12. John 18:38 records Pilate's relativistic question: "What is truth?" reflecting moral ambiguity.
13. 2 Timothy 4:10 mentions Demas, who abandoned Paul "having loved this present world."
14. 1 Samuel 8 shows Israel demanding a king, preferring cultural conformity over divine leadership.
15. Acts 17:21 notes the Athenians' obsession with "telling or hearing something new," symbolic of mystical wanderers.
16. Numbers 20:10-12 records Moses' impulsive striking of the rock, showing wounded activism misrepresenting God.
17. Jonah 4 displays Jonah's anger at God's mercy, reflecting the hurt activist's struggle.
18. Matthew 13:20-21 explains the rocky soil—those who receive the Word with joy but fall away under trial.
19. Galatians 1:6-9 confronts the Judaizers, showing the danger of adding works to the Gospel.
20. Galatians 2:11-14 recounts Paul's public

confrontation of Peter's hypocrisy concerning Gentile believers.
21. John 20:24–29 shows Thomas's doubt addressed not with rebuke, but with tangible proof of Christ's wounds.
22. Matthew 11:3 portrays John the Baptist's honest doubt while imprisoned, asking if Jesus is truly the One.
23. Acts 5:1–11 narrates the deception of Ananias and Sapphira, spiritual manipulators within the early Church.
24. John 6:26–66 captures the thinning of the crowd when Jesus preached the cost of true discipleship.
25. John 8:1–11 recounts Jesus' merciful yet convicting engagement with the adulterous woman and her accusers.
26. 1 Corinthians 4:7 reminds believers that all they have is received from God, preserving humility in discernment.
27. 2 Timothy 4:16 records Paul's loneliness as many abandoned him, yet he remained faithful.
28. Colossians 4:6 exhorts believers to speak "with grace, seasoned with salt," balancing clarity and compassion.
29. Romans 9:2 shows Paul's great sorrow for unbelieving Israel, modeling intercessory burden for the lost.
30. John 6:66–67 captures Jesus' response to those who walkaway—not retreat, but reaffirmation of truth.
31. 1 John 2:19 teaches that those who depart from truth reveal they were never truly part of it.
32. 1 Corinthians 13:2 warns that knowledge without love is nothing.
33. 1 Peter 4:11 commands that whoever speaks should speak as one "speaking the oracles of God."

34. Matthew 24:12-13 warns that in the last days, "because iniquity shall abound, the love of many shall wax cold," but the faithful will endure.
35. Luke 15:20 shows the Father's heart—seeing the prodigal "a long way off," moved with compassion to run toward him.

Chapter 8: Recovering Servant Leadership

1. Philippians 2:7 describes Christ "taking the form of a servant" and humbling Himself.
2. Acts 17:6 records how the early Christians were accused of "turning the world upside down."
3. John 13:4-5 depicts Jesus rising from the table to wash His disciples' feet, embodying true leadership.
4. John 13:14 is Jesus' command that His disciples must also wash one another's feet.
5. Acts 20:19 shows Paul's leadership marked by "all humility and with tears and with trials."
6. 1 Peter 5:2-3 exhorts elders to shepherd "not domineering over those in your charge, but being examples."
7. James 3:1 warns that teachers will be judged more strictly.
8. John 10:12-13 warns about the hired hand who abandons the sheep when danger comes.
9. 1 Timothy 3 outlines the qualifications of elders and deacons, emphasizing character over charisma.
10. Romans 9:2 expresses Paul's "great heaviness and continual sorrow" for the lost.
11. Matthew 20:26-28 declares that greatness in the Kingdom comes through serving others.
12. Hebrews 12:6 states that the Lord disciplines those He loves.

13. 2 Samuel 12:13 records David's repentant confession after Nathan's rebuke.
14. Galatians 2:11 recounts Paul's public rebuke of Peter for compromising the Gospel.
15. Proverbs 12:15 says a wise man listens to advice, while the fool is right in his own eyes.
16. Philippians 2:5–8 exhorts believers to have the mind of Christ, who humbled Himself to the point of death.
17. John 5:19 shows Jesus doing nothing of His own accord, but only what He sees the Father doing.
18. Hebrews 5:8 teaches that Jesus "learned obedience through what He suffered."
19. Philippians 2:12 urges believers to "work out your own salvation with fear and trembling."
20. Galatians 5:22–23 lists the fruit of the Spirit as the defining marks of Christian maturity.
21. Matthew 25:21 records Jesus' commendation: "Well done, good and faithful servant."
22. Matthew 20:28 affirms that the Son of Man came "not to be served but to serve."
23. John 13:14 repeats Jesus' charge that His disciples must imitate His servant-hearted example.
24. Matthew 25:21 again emphasizes that faithfulness, not fame, is what Christ commends.
25. John 13:4–5 (repeated) anchors the image of Christ's leadership as foot-washing, not fame-seeking.

Chapter 9: A Kingdom Without Walls

1. Matthew 28:19 records Christ's command to "make disciples of all nations."
2. John 17:21 captures Jesus' prayer that His followers "may all be one."

3. Romans 14:1 urges believers to accept one another without quarrelling over disputable matters.
4. Galatians 1:6 warns against turning to "a different gospel," emphasizing Gospel purity over additions.
5. John 13:35 declares that the world will know Christ's disciples "if ye have love one to another."
6. Ephesians 2:14–16 teaches that Christ "broke down the dividing wall of hostility" through His death.
7. Ephesians 4:2–3 exhorts believers to maintain unity "with all humility and gentleness... through the bond of peace."
8. 1 Corinthians 1:12–13 rebukes sectarianism: "Is Christ divided?"
9. Philippians 3:20 reminds believers that "our conversation [citizenship] is in heaven."
10. Romans 1:16 defines the Gospel as" the power of God unto salvation to every one that believeth."
11. John 13:35 (repeated) underscores the primary mark of discipleship: love among believers.
12. Romans 1:16 (repeated) again highlights that the Gospel, not theological systems, is the means of salvation.

Chapter 10: A Watchman's Call to the Remnant

1. Ezekiel 33:7 – God commissions Ezekiel as a Watchman to hear His word and give warning.
2. Ezekiel 33:8 – The Watchman's accountability: failure to warn results in blood guilt.
3. 1 Kings 19:18 – God reminds Elijah that He has preserved a faithful remnant who have not bowed to Baal.
4. Revelation 3:1–2 – Christ's warning to the church in Sardis: a reputation for life, but spiritual death; the call to wake up and strengthen what remains.

5. Revelation 3:4 – Christ commends the faithful few in Sardis who have not soiled their garments.
6. John 1:14 – Jesus is described as full of grace and truth, the embodiment of God's Word.
7. 2 Timothy 4:2 – Paul exhorts Timothy to preach the Word faithfully in all seasons, with patience and teaching.
8. Ezekiel 33:6 – The Watchman's burden: if he fails to sound the warning, the blood is required at his hand.
9. Revelation 3:2 (repeated for emphasis) – Christ's charge to be watchful and strengthen what remains.
10. John 13:35 – Love for one another is the distinguishing mark of Christ's disciples.

Bibliography

Books & Print Publications

Beaty, Katelyn. *Celebrities for Jesus: How Personas, Platforms, and Profits Are Hurting the Church.* Brazos Press, 2022.

Grudem, Wayne. *Systematic Theology: An Introduction to Biblical Doctrine.* Zondervan, 1994.

MacArthur, John. *The Truth War: Fighting for Certainty in an Age of Deception.* Thomas Nelson, 2007.

Noll, Mark. *Turning Points: Decisive Moments in the History of Christianity.* Baker Academic, 2000.

Ortlund, Gavin. *Finding the Right Hills to Die On: The Case for Theological Triage.* Crossway, 2020.

Packer, J.I. *Knowing God.* Downers Grove, IL: InterVarsity Press, 1973.

Schaeffer, Francis A. *The Mark of the Christian.* InterVarsity Press, 1970.

Schaff, Philip. *The Creeds of Christendom.* Harper & Row, 1877.

Sire, James W. *The Universe Next Door: A Basic Worldview Catalog.* InterVarsity Press, 2009.

Sproul, R.C. *Scripture Alone: The Evangelical Doctrine.* P&R Publishing, 2005.

Strauch, Alexander. *Biblical Eldership: An Urgent Call to Restore Biblical Church Leadership.* Lewis and Roth, 1995.

Tozer, A.W. *The Pursuit of God.* Christian Publications, 1948.

Vanhoozer, Kevin J. *Is There a Meaning in This Text? The Bible, the Reader, and the Morality of Literary Knowledge.* Zondervan, 1998.

Creeds & Historical Documents

"**The Nicene Creed.**" Council of Nicaea, AD 325.
"**The Apostles' Creed.**" Early Christian statement of faith, traditionally dated to the 2nd century.
"**The Chalcedonian Definition.**" Council of Chalcedon, AD 451.
"**The Westminster Confession of Faith.**" Church of England, 1646.
"**The Chicago Statement on Biblical Inerrancy.**" International Council on Biblical Inerrancy, 1978.

Web Sources

Crossway.org – Resources on doctrinal triage and theological essentials. Accessed April 20, 2025. https://www.crossway.org

DesiringGod.org – Articles and sermons on biblical unity and church leadership. Accessed April 20, 2025. https://www.desiringgod.org

The Gospel Coalition – Essays on hermeneutics, ecclesiology, and church culture. Accessed April 20, 2025. https://www.thegospelcoalition.org

IVPress.com – Author archives and theological resources. Accessed April 20, 2025. https://www.ivpress.com

Ligonier.org – Resources by R.C. Sproul and others on sola Scriptura. Accessed April 20, 2025. https://www.ligonier.org

About the Author

Juel Mendez is a former United States Marine, seasoned Federal Agent, and licensed Private Investigator with over 25 years of combined experience in law enforcement, intelligence, global operations, entrepreneurship, and spiritual discernment.

His journey began with a four-year tour in the U.S. Marine Corps, where he developed the discipline and endurance that would carry him through the next phase of his life in law enforcement. From Police Officer to Special Deputy to Federal Agent, he climbed the ranks with determination and resolve. In his federal role, he conducted international operations that brought him face-to-face with complex realities across the globe—visiting countries such as Spain, France, Germany, Greece, the United Kingdom, Denmark, Norway, Turkey, India, Israel, Iraq, Iran, and several African nations. These experiences exposed him to both the beauty and the brokenness of the world—and stirred in him a deeper hunger for truth.

Following health challenges that ended his federal service, he turned to entrepreneurship, founding several brands—some successful, others instructive in failure. Yet through every season, his pursuit of truth remained at the center. Each chapter of his journey has shaped his voice: investigative, reflective, and unwavering.

Now, after decades of training, field experience, and God-given wisdom, he has recognized his true calling—apologetics. He is devoted to defending biblical truth in a time of spiritual confusion, through both non-fiction and allegorical storytelling. His upcoming works include The Scroll of the Seven Watchtowers, a prophetic allegory that explores spiritual awakening through layered symbolism and scriptural reflection.

Through his writing, Juel invites readers into the tension between deception and discernment. He writes not merely to inform, but to awaken. His voice carries the weight of a man who has seen systems falter, ideologies fail, and truth buried—yet still believes redemption is possible. With every page, he calls the reader to examine the world more carefully, and to return to the One who holds the ultimate answer.

Also by

The Watchman's Field Manual

A practical guide for those called to discernment and intercession. Designed as a training tool for the vigilant believer, this manual outlines the postures, prayers, and principles of a biblical watchman.

Unity Companion

A devotional and doctrinal companion designed to walk alongside A House Divided. It offers Scripture meditations, unity practices, and personal reflection prompts for those contending for truth in love.

The Watchman's Codex

A visual and theological companion to A House Divided, exploring the thirteen Faces of Deception and the tools of spiritual discernment through symbols, Scripture, and strategic insight.

Available at:

juelmendez.com/watchman-voice-for-truth

The Watchman's Handbook (eBook Exclusive)

A tactical resource for field application, equipping modern watchmen with biblical responses to doctrinal confusion, cultural compromise, and spiritual deception.

The Concordance of Deception (eBook Exclusive)

A searchable reference of modern distortions—defined and diagnosed through Scripture. This concordance names the false virtues, spiritual counterfeits, and doctrinal trends that undermine truth in the name of tolerance.

Accessible at:

juelmendez.com/books-christian-apologetics

To follow Juel's latest writings, teaching tools, and projects,

Visit:

www.juelmendez.com and join the Watchman's Circle.

www.ingramcontent.com/pod-product-compliance
Lightning Source LLC
Chambersburg PA
CBHW022203090526
44583CB00012BA/258